BANISH BURNOUT TOOLKIT

Praise for Janice's *Banish Burnout Toolkit*

"At last, a stress management book that is practical and not theoretical – written by a stress management expert, who knows what she is talking about."

— **Patricia Fripp,** Past President, National Speakers Association, Executive Speech Coach, Keynote Speaker, and Author of *World Class Speaking: The Ultimate Guide to Presenting, Marketing and Profiting Like a Champion*

"Janice Litvin takes an ageless truth (pause before reacting) and weaves it into a timely message for surviving and growing during these stressful times. The *Banish Burnout Toolkit* is user friendly and practical. I recommend it most highly."

— **Jim Purcell,** Former CEO, Blue Cross & Blue Shield of RI; Founder of Returns on Wellbeing Institute

"If you're seeking sanity in an unprecedented time, look no further. Janice Litvin's *Banish Burnout Toolkit* is an excellent step-by-step guide to counter stress and burnout, filled with examples and exercises that are both relatable and actionable. I highly recommend it!"

— **Laura Putnam,** Author of *Workplace Wellness That Works* and CEO, Founder of Motion Infusion

"Stress and burnout are at all-time highs. We can all benefit from the practical and actionable techniques in the *Banish Burnout Toolkit.* Janice provides practices we can incorporate into our daily lives, so we can be more fulfilled, happier, and healthier."

— **Mari Ryan, MBA, MHP, CWP,** CEO/Founder of Advancing Wellness and Award-winning author of *The Thriving Hive: How People Centric Workplaces Ignite Engagement and Fuel Results*

"Changing and developing new habits can be difficult. This workbook takes the complex and sometimes invisible aspects that make change difficult and breaks them down into easily and immediately accessible exercises. It allows the reader to ask deeply valuable questions to identify and remove emotional blocks, which are often hidden. That makes for a combination of simplicity and removing obstacles from the roots, which is absolutely brilliant!"

— **Reut Schwartz-Hebron,** Expert in Neuroscience and Difficult Change and Author of *The Art and Science of Changing People Who Don't Want to Change*

"Janice Litvin's *Banish Burnout Toolkit* is an incredibly valuable resource for managing stress and burnout! Importantly she addresses how early hurtful messages lead to taking things personally, overreacting and self-criticizing. The *Banish Burnout Toolkit* shows you how to break the cycle of self-doubt, which can cause reduced performance and productivity. The Stop and Audit exercises — especially the Reality Spin reframes — provide opportunities for developing new choices for responding to old triggers."

> — **Elayne Savage, PhD,** Practicing Psychotherapist, Workplace Coach and Author of *Don't Take It Personally! The Art of Dealing with Rejection*

"Stress comes in many forms and, unfortunately, is not going to disappear. What makes the difference in our lives is how we react to stress. In her *Banish Burnout Toolkit*. Janice Litvin provides practical ideas and suggestions that we can implement that will change how we think about and deal with stress. And, ultimately, Banish Burnout."

> — **Susan Roane,** Keynote Speaker, The Mingling Maven® and Author of *How to Work a Room* and *The Secrets of Savvy Networking*

"Janice Litvin is the go-to person when it comes to Wellness in the Workplace. Her workbook, *Banish Burnout Toolkit* is packed with real life, how-to and easy-to-implement action steps to eliminate the stress and tension in your life. Her section on practicing self-care has already made an impact on my life. It is a great resource guide which I am recommending to my network!"

> — **Arnold Sanow, MBA, CSP,** Speaker and Author of *Get Along with Anyone, Anytime, Anywhere*

"I am proud to brandish my *Banish Burnout Toolkit* workbook for all to see. It is a wonderful compendium that blends stories with stats, physiology and psychology, relates great stories of the author's and others' who've struggled before succeeding in banishing stress and regaining a balanced life. This workbook contains my favorite kinds of exercises…ones I can complete while remaining seated! Janice brings wisdom derived from her worlds of high-tech and home life to bear in this well organized, logical workbook that will simultaneously enhance the quality of your life even as it extends yours. This workbook works! Thank you, Janice for this companion to usher us through the pandemic into a brighter future free from stress."

> — **Craig Harrison,** Speaker, Founder, Expressions Of Excellence and Author of *Stellar Service! Merge WOW with NOW to Create Customers for Life*

"*Banish Burnout Toolkit* by Janice Litvin, Workplace Wellness Speaker, is just what the doctor ordered! It provides the reader with a practical and valuable collection of tools, tips, and techniques for reducing overwhelm and stress so as to enhance both their wellbeing and productivity. After reading this book cover-to-cover, I am feeling less stressed already. Dealing with stress is not an event, but a process -- and not a destination, but a journey. I am very glad to have Litvin's book to carry with me along the way."

> — **Todd Cherches,** CEO of Big Blue Gumball, and Author of *VisuaLeadership: Leveraging the Power of Visual Thinking in Leadership and in Life*

Whether you think you are on the road to burnout or not, in our 24/7 culture, each of us is susceptible in some way(s). In the Banish Burnout Toolkit, Janice Litvin offers comprehensive and practical strategies that not only minimize your risk of actually burning out, but which can enhance your life, daily and nightly. The more you deal with stress during your waking hours, the more you set the stage for an essential good night's sleep. Thank you, Janice, for empowering people to move towards health and well-being, both essential for success and joy.

— **Nancy H. Rothstein,** MBA, The Sleep Ambassador®

"Pay attention to the advice in this comprehensive workbook. Use the tool to conduct an honest self-audit and Janice's S.T.O.P. process to your life. You will be so glad you did."

— **Neen James,** Keynote Speaker and Author of *Attention Pays*

"I promise you that Janice Litvin has created a work that will influence your business, home, and personal life with a much needed, extremely timely book in *Banish Burnout Toolkit.* For the WFH parent like me, I'd say Tool #5 regarding setting healthy boundaries at home is of the essence to every reader this day and time, along with so many other powerful concepts within. I highly endorse this great workbook, as well as Janice as an authority on the subject of reducing stress, an author, and a wonderful speaker."

— **Jason Hewlett,** Author of *The Promise to The One*, Hall of Fame Speaker, Award-Winning Entertainer

"Want a stress management book that offers concrete strategies and practical solutions for those who lead and work in a high-paced environment? Read *Banish Burnout Toolkit* to negotiate work and drive winning performance with everyone on your team."

— **Linda Swindling, JD, CSP,** Negotiation Expert and Author of *Ask Outrageously: The Secret to Getting What You Really Want!*

"Stress isn't going away. The *Banish Burnout Toolkit* is a great resource for anyone looking to better manage their stress. The workbook is filled with great insights and practical ways to reflect, assess, and make any adjustments."

— **Allison Tabor,** Executive Coach, Professional Speaker, Facilitator and Bestselling Author of *Work Your ASSets Off, Stop Working So Hard in Business and in Life*

"We all have been "told" the best ways to manage stress. So, why don't the strategies that work for others work for you? The answer is simple, you are not "them." Janice Litvin's *Banish Burnout Toolkit* provides a practical approach that will enable you to create concrete stress management solutions that work best for you."

— **Susan Schwartz,** Executive and Organizational Coach, Trainer, and Author of *Creating a Greater Whole: A Project Manager's Guide to Becoming a Leader*

BANISH BURNOUT TOOLKIT

Based on the popular
Banish Burnout: Move from Stress to Success
Workshops and Programs

by Janice Litvin

Printed in the United States of America

First Printing, 2020
ISBN: 978-1-7349242-6-8 (Paperback)
ISBN: 978-1-7349242-7-5 (eBook – Kindle)
ISBN: 978-1-7349242-8-2 (eBook - Portable Document Format)

Library of Congress Control Number: 2020949000

 A Page Beyond LLC
Fishers, IN 46037
www.APageBeyond.com

Ordering Information:

Special discounts are available on quantity purchases by corporations, associations, and others who purchase directly from the author. Contact Janice@JaniceLitvin.com for details.

Disclaimer:

Care has been taken to confirm the accuracy of the information presented and to describe generally accepted practices. However, the author, editor, and publisher are not responsible for errors or omissions or for any consequences from application of the information in this workbook, and make no warranty, express or implied, with respect to the contents of the publication.

The materials provided in this workbook are for educational purposes only and are not intended to replace, be a substitute for, or to be construed as providing medical, psychological, or psychiatric treatment. The author is not a psychologist, psychiatrist, nor medical doctor.

The advice and strategies contained herein may not be suitable for your situation. You should consult with a professional where appropriate. If you are in acute distress, anxiety, or depression, or thinking about harming yourself or others, seek professional help immediately.

Dedication

To my parents, Sylvia & Robert Isaac Schooler,
who always taught me to reach for the stars and never give up.

Table of Contents

Foreword

Stress is an inevitable, and necessary part of life, but it can be motivating or destructive.

The negative impact that stress and burnout have on our health, happiness, and productivity is well-documented and widely accepted. Stressors can lead to unhealthy choices: stress-eating, depression-fueled lethargy, and the abuse of drugs, alcohol, and nicotine.

In the *Banish Burnout Toolkit*, Janice Litvin combines her passion, experience, and expertise for health and wellbeing to deliver an easy-to-use, easy-to-follow compendium of exercises, activities and information to help manage stress, modify maladaptive thinking, and mitigate burnout.

She brings it all together, leveraging key components of Cognitive Behavioral Therapy, Rational Emotive Therapy, and Mindfulness.

Rick Hecht, LMFT
Behavioral Health and Employee Wellness Strategist
Healthcare Industry Leader

Introduction

Welcome to the ***Banish Burnout Toolkit,*** the workbook based on my ***Banish Burnout: Move from Stress to Success*** program that helps you change the way you react to stress, from the inside out.

As you move through the exercises in this workbook, you will learn how your thoughts control your feelings and impact your behavior, and your habits affect your thoughts. That knowledge will help you banish burnout!

This workbook reflects my 20+ years in human resources as a technology recruiter, my experience working in the IT department at three different companies, my studies of psychology, and my experience changing my behavior in response to stress using cognitive behavior therapy.

One of the core concepts underlying this workbook and my program is the notion that learning to manage stress will enable you to prevent burnout and help you thrive at work.

Viktor Frankl (1905 – 1997), Austrian Holocaust survivor, neurologist and psychiatrist, and author of *Man's Search for Meaning,* and many other books, taught that it is more important to focus on how we respond to stress, rather than the stress, itself.

That is what I want you to learn, that the way you react to stress is under your control. Many people think someone or something causes them to experience some extreme emotion like anger. The *stressor or incident* definitely has an impact, but the way you react is up to you. You can change your thoughts and emotions in reaction to a stressor or situation.

Let's face it. We all feel too much stress from time to time. Our emotional reactions are part of a normal human response. But here are two key questions for you to consider about the way you react: *how low do you go and how long do you stay there*? In other words, is your level of anger commensurate with the situation? And for how long do you let the negative feelings linger? If someone cuts you off in traffic how upset do you get? It is normal to have an emotional reaction when someone is rude or critical, or annoys you in some way, especially at work. But do you let those emotions control you so that you over-react or become combative? Do you stay "moody" or upset for a very long time?

The answers to these questions and others you will address in this workbook will help you identify whether or not you may be headed towards burnout and how to change course.

Dr. Albert Ellis, considered the father of cognitive behavior therapy, said that cognitive behavior therapy is problem-focused and action-oriented.

That is how I have developed my model of the **Banish Burnout Toolkit**, by giving you action-oriented tools to help you uncover your reactions to stress and learn to how to re-script your reactions. Ellis taught that information-processing and coping mechanisms are the keys to healing.

That is what I have provided in this workbook: six tools, which include how to identify your typical stress responses and where they came from, learning how to change them, recognizing and releasing your life-long behavior patterns, practicing self-care and setting boundaries in your relationships at work and at home. In addition, you'll be encouraged to enlist the support of an accountability buddy.

All you need is awareness, your imagination, and the willingness to change. That is how you take charge and take control to let go of the power stress has over you. You will be happier, more productive, and you will *banish burnout*.

Tool #1:
S-T-O-P and Audit to Build Awareness

The key to managing stress and banishing burnout is to change your behavior. And the first step to any behavior change is building awareness. You cannot make any change without it.

This tool provides exercises that help you build the awareness you need in order to recognize your intense responses to stress, and then to adopt healthier coping strategies.

You'll begin by learning the **S-T-O-P** process and then follow it up by conducting a **Stress Audit**. The **S-T-O-P** process and the **Stress Audit** fit together as one.

Image © MMXX by Janice Litvin

Learn to S-T-O-P

Rollo May (1909 – 1994), psychiatrist and author of *Man's Search for Himself,* taught that human freedom comes from the ability to pause so that you can think before you respond, and breathe before you react. That is exactly what the first step of **Tool #1** is all about, not reacting automatically, but rather, pausing and then choosing the response you wish to make.

The S-T-O-P concept was developed by Jon Kabat-Zinn, considered to be the father of modern-day mindfulness. S-T-O-P is a powerful method for calming yourself in the face of stress. Mindfulness and meditation practices serve to train you to become aware of your thoughts and internal reactions.

S-T-O-P stands for Stop, Take a Breath, Observe, and then Proceed.

This process underlies the whole **Banish Burnout Toolkit** because in order to successfully change your behavior, you must pay attention to how you are feeling in the moment when you are experiencing a reaction to stress.

You can practice **S-T-O-P** at any time of the day or night when you are faced with a stressful situation. It requires no fancy body stance or position. All you have to do is learn how to get in the practice of **S-T-O-P**-ping whenever you are upset.

I have trained myself to **S-T-O-P** in the midst of a stressful moment, and it has made a significant difference in my life and in my ability to be more effective at work. With practice, you will find that your ability to short circuit intense stress responses will grow stronger and will occur quicker and quicker, until one day you are **S-T-O-P**-ping yourself as soon as you get upset.

That is not to say, you will never react emotionally. You would not be human if you didn't. However, you will catch yourself in the act of over-reacting much sooner, and then you will ease the tension and eventually remove it much sooner, in the moment.

This is how the **S-T-O-P** process works.

S - Stop

The first part, the **Stop** step, is merely a trick to get yourself to pay attention to how you are feeling. Quite simply, you stop what you are thinking, feeling, or saying, just for a moment. This causes you to interrupt negative thoughts building up to extreme feelings that cause extreme behavior.

T - Take-a-Breath

The second step, **Take-a-Breath**, is a critical precursor to awareness. Take a very deep cleansing breath or two. Deep breathing signals the parasympathetic nervous system to calm the body down and change your whole state of mind, allowing you to begin thinking more clearly.

In the future, when you encounter a stressful situation, you will be able to take 60 seconds to take a deep breath to regulate your breathing and emotions, even if you don't have time to perform the complete **Stress Audit**, described in the next section.

O - Observe

The *Observe* step is **where the actual Stress Audit comes in**. You will focus your awareness on what you are thinking, feeling, and saying, paying close attention to what is going on outside and inside of you. As soon as possible, take the time to step back and observe your reaction to the stressful experience or whatever is causing your negative thoughts or feelings

Please note that this step, *Observe,* is the foundation of the **Stress Audit**, the next part of this tool. You can apply this part of the process quickly in response to an immediate event, such as a brush with a bad driver. Or you can apply it in the written **Stress Audit** that follows, where you will take more time to analyze your responses to momentary stressors or incidents or possible ongoing stressful situations, or even anxieties about a difficult encounter you are anticipating in the future.

Whether you *Observe* your responses immediately in a stressful moment or reflect upon them later, this part of the **S-T-O-P** process gives you a wealth of information about yourself that will be essential to changing your behavior.

P - Proceed

As the name infers, the ***Proceed*** step means that you simply proceed, or go on about your day, while acknowledging how you are feeling. You will use the information you discovered when you took the time to *Observe* your responses. Then you can consciously decide how you want to move on. When you ***Proceed***, you acknowledge that the stressor is over, that you've paid full attention to your feelings, and that now, you can let it all go, cleansing your thoughts of negativity. You can even choose to smile at yourself.

In some cases, you may prefer to get away from a stressful situation so that you can take a brief respite to collect yourself and decide how you wish to behave in the moment. You may need to leave temporarily, and then return to the situation, or you may decide to remove yourself altogether.

For example, one of my clients recounted attending a party where, upon entry, she was bombarded with a rude criticism by a friend. Instead of arguing, she chose to leave, take a walk around the block to settle herself, process what had happened, and then return to the party, remaining civil to the friend. This is **S-T-O-P** in action. She remembered having a nice time because she had taken the time to **S-T-O-P** and check her emotions.

Conduct Your Stress Audit

As you learned in the previous discussion of the **S-T-O-P** process, the *Observe* step is the fundamental underpinning of the **Stress Audit**. The purpose of the **Stress Audit** is to uncover and focus on possible pent-up feelings in reaction to something that has happened, a stressor, or incident of some sort. It could stem from something small, such as being on hold too long for technical support, or something big, like a major disagreement or disappointment at work.

It is important to note that pushing down and ignoring feelings leads to emotional outbursts later. So the value of the stress audit is to give your feelings a place to exist.

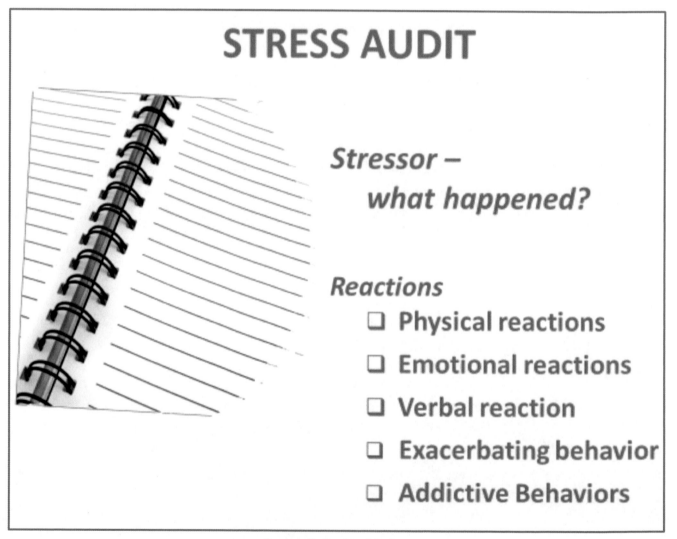

Image © Janice Litvin

The **Stress Audit** is fairly easy to complete. You simply ask yourself, "How am I feeling right now in this moment?" as soon as you can after a stressful incident. In some cases, such as when you are alone in your parked car after having over-reacted to someone or something happened, you will be able to audit your feelings in the immediate moment. At other times, like when you are in a work meeting, you will probably not be able to start your **Stress Audit** until sometime after the meeting. But as soon as possible after the event, try to start your audit, either at your desk or in your break area or a quiet room.

Example

Stressor / inciting incident:	disagreement at work
My physical reactions:	tight jaw, neck or shoulders, knots in the stomach, headache, elevated heart rate, or shallow breathing
My emotional reactions:	anger, frustration, hurt, resentment, sadness
My verbal reactions:	arguing, complaining, negativity
Exacerbating behavior:	letting the complaining go on too long and with much intensity
Possible addictive behaviors:	overeating or excessive use of alcohol, drugs, or cigarettes, smoking, shopping, screen time, or any other type of avoidance behavior including procrastination or overwork

Note: Addiction is rather a complex subject and is not the focus of this book. However, I include it here because it is important to point out that addiction is a person's unconscious attempt to escape pain, according to Dr. Gabor Mate, Hungarian-born Canadian physician, who specializes in childhood development and trauma. What I want is for you to let the feelings out so that you can learn to manage them. You don't have to repress them, but rather connect to them in a healthy way. You will learn more about uncovering your emotions in **Tool #3 Unpack Your Emotional Baggage**, and then communicating your needs in **Tool #5 Set Healthy Boundaries.**

So, the point of including Addiction in the Stress Audit is just to make you aware of your behavior so you can begin to identify what habits you may want to change. If you or one of your employees is slipping into a serious addiction, I recommend seeking help from a mental health professional. Many large companies have access to an EAP (Employee Assistance Program) that provides anonymous mental health resources.

Exercise

Write out something upsetting that happened recently, big or small. Then write your reactions, including the level of intensity you felt.

What happened? Describe the stressor or inciting incident.

_____

_____

_____

_____

_____

Physical: How did you react physically?

_____

_____

_____

_____

Emotional: How did you react emotionally?

_____

_____

_____

_____

Verbal: What did you say?

_____

_____

_____

_____

Exacerbating behavior: How upset did you get and how long did you stay there?

_____

_____

_____

_____

_____

Possible Addictive Behaviors. What avoidance behavior did you engage in, if any?

If you are the type of person who engages in addictive behavior, this step will be critical. Learning how to cope without the addiction is a very difficult change to make, but it is possible with practice and more practice. In extreme cases, you may want to engage a professional.

_____

_____

_____

_____

_____

What did you learn from this exercise?

_____

_____

_____

_____

_____

_____

_____

_____

_____

S-T-O-P and Audit

Tool #2:
Know Your Stress - Spin Your Stress

In **Tool #1** you began the process of leaning into automatic reactions, so that you can raise your awareness about how you think, feel, and behave when faced with a stressful situation or incident. Using **Tool #2** you will expand that awareness to identify the habitual ways you respond to stress, particularly the thought and behavior patterns you may have developed to cope with stressors. Your thoughts control your feelings and impact your behavior. When this behavior becomes a pattern, suddenly you have developed a habit. I am going to teach you how to understand where those patterns came from and then how to change them to give you freedom over your negative thoughts.

Neural Pathways

Where do our behavior patterns come from? It is important to understand that the way we think, behave and act are rooted in patterns of behavior developed long ago. For example, you were likely taught as a child to say "Thank you," every time someone did or said something nice to you. Then in response they said, "You're welcome." That is a polite behavior pattern many people were taught.

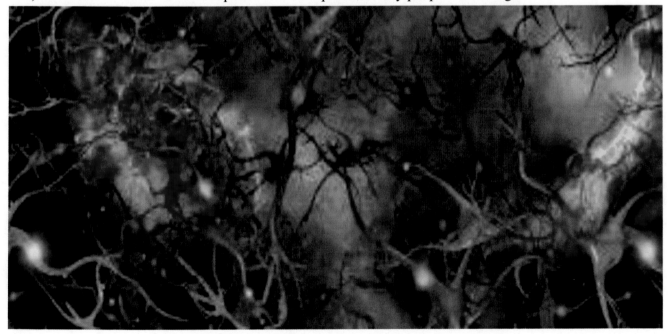

Image by Shutterstock.com. Used under Standard License.

Mixed in with polite behavior were other behavior patterns that may not have been so nice. Interestingly, our patterns of behavior (including patterns of reacting to stressful events) came from either role modelling we observed by our parents or teachers, or from the way parents treated us or other people. You will dig deeper into the source of your behavior patterns in **Tool #3 Unpack Your Emotional Baggage**. For now, the point is to show you how those patterns got etched into your brain and became patterns.

They got cemented, so to speak, in your brain in an area that neuroscientists call, *neural pathways*. They are like a path on the highway. They are the communication network for your brain. Believe it or not, these pathways can be re-programmed to set up new patterns. That is one of the important lessons I am going to teach you in this workbook, how to uncover the patterns of your neural pathways so that you can re-program them. This is how you will change your behavior and set up new ways of thinking and behaving in reaction to stress, so that you can *banish burnout*.

The first step is to identify your typical **Stress Response Patterns**. The second step will be to apply a rational approach to change those patterns through the **Reality Spin**.

Understand Typical Stress Response Patterns and the Reality Spin

When something goes wrong during your day, be it a computer glitch that stops you from accomplishing your work, or a car that won't start when you need to get to work, do you tend to have a usual response, like,

- *Life is so unfair.*
- *Why do these problems always happen to me?*
- *My boss doesn't like me, and I can't stand her.*

In the case of your car not starting, maybe you go to an extreme reaction, like thinking you'll have to buy a whole new car, instead of just a new battery.

When we get upset, it is very common to lose control over our emotions. We cannot really think clearly. Have you ever said to yourself, "I was so angry, I couldn't think straight"? Or, after an argument, have you ever thought, "I wish I had said…"? This is the common reaction in which we allow the fear center of our brain, the *amygdala,* to take control.

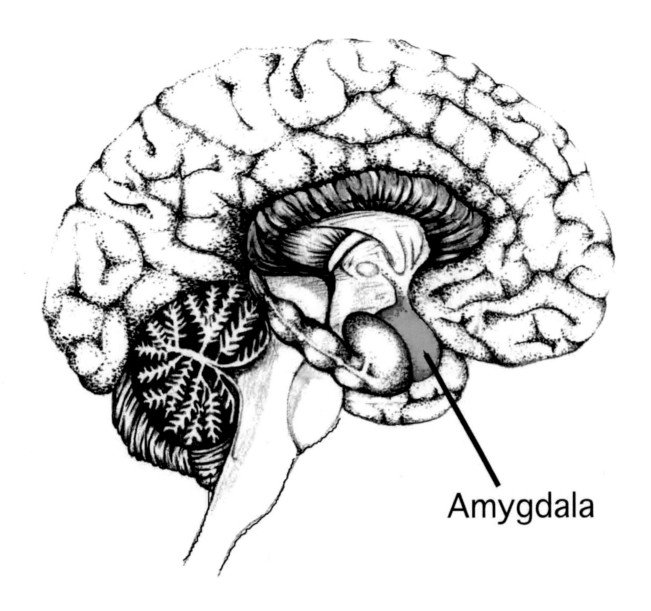

Amygdala

"Amygdala" by Memory Loss Online on Wikimedia Commons. Used under Creative Commons CC0 1.0 License.

This process is commonly referred to as *distorted thinking*. Your reactions tend to become exaggerated over-reactions or over-generalizations. This type of reaction is referred to as a *cognitive distortion, cognitive* meaning *the act of thinking or reasoning*. In other words, cognitive distortions are essentially irrational, inaccurate, or false beliefs or thought patterns.

We all turn to them upon occasion. We all have our personal irrational or unrealistic responses that may pop up from time to time. Your goal throughout this tool is to recognize your own individual response patterns.

There are a variety of common cognitive distortions that can arise when stressed. Some people immediately jump to conclusions, while others focus instantly on negative events, ignoring positive ones, and still others catastrophize.

We are going to focus on three common **Stress Response Patterns**:

- Over-reaction / exaggeration
- Over-generalization
- "Should" statements

The second part of this tool teaches you how to change your reaction to the stressor. In order to combat distorted thinking, we need to learn to apply rational arguments to stressful situations. We do that through a technique I call the **Reality Spin**.

In technical terms this is called *cognitive restructuring* or *cognitive reframing*. The goal of this process is to challenge your distorted thinking and then convert those thoughts into a more realistic, rational response.

This is where the magic of behavior change happens. With focus and practice, you get better and better at catching yourself in the act of over-reacting and asking yourself, "is this level of anger commensurate with what is happening?" Often the answer is *no*, and then in the moment you can say to yourself, "It is not worth getting this upset over something so minor. I am going to stop this *stinking thinking* and make a decision to put myself in a better, happier mood." At first it may not happen until after the incident or

situation. But eventually you will start to catch yourself in the act sooner and sooner, as discussed earlier in the discussion of the **S-T-O-P** exercise in **Tool #1**.

This process of stopping yourself is a very powerful step and allows you to engage your Prefrontal Cortex, the analytical, reasoning, executive functioning part of the brain.

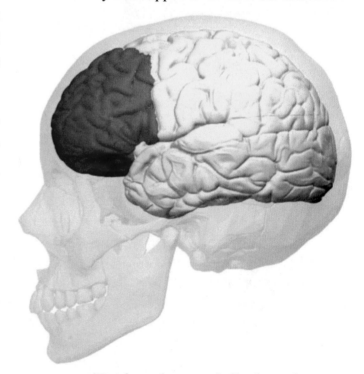

"Prefrontal cortex (left) - lateral view" by Database Center for Life Science (DBCLS) CC BY-SA 2.1 jp

Here are some suggested questions to ask yourself in order to apply the **Reality Spin** or to reframe a situation, so you can snap yourself out of emotional turmoil and replace it with calming clarity and logic:

- *Am I responding emotionally or rationally?*
- *Am I over-reacting?*
- *What evidence is there that my response is accurate?*
- *What evidence is there that my response is appropriate?*
- *What else could be going on to exacerbate my emotions?*
- *Am I really worried or upset about something else?*
- *Is there another way to interpret this situation?*
- *What's the worst that can happen?*
- *Is this really a black-and-white situation, or are there shades of grey?*

This has worked for me over and over again. If I can do it, so can you.

Example

In the box below you can see how the **Reality Spin** can be applied to a distorted stress response in the case of a person whose car won't start on a cold morning.

Stress Response	*Reality Spin*
My car won't start! OMG, I'm going to be so late for work. What am I going to do? I'm going to have to get rid of it and buy another car!	*My car won't start! Okay. Stuff happens. What could be the problem? And what's the worst that can happen? Maybe it's the battery. My neighbor (or partner) can give me a jump start, or I'll have it towed to a mechanic and call for a ride from there. Meanwhile I'll text the boss and let her know what is happening.*

Recognize Over-Reaction and Exaggeration

Now that you've seen an overview of **Stress Response Patterns** and the **Reality Spin** concept, it's time to take a closer look at common distortions in your thinking, that make it more difficult to manage your stress. This section focuses on one set of common distortions, **over-reaction and exaggeration**.

Photo by Icons 8 Team on Unsplash. Used under Standard License.

Do you get very angry or upset at the littlest annoyance or do you know someone who does?

Over-reacting is about blowing things out of proportion, becoming histrionic or overly dramatic. Exaggerations are sometimes referred to as "catastrophizing," because we tend to respond to a minor incident as though it were a major catastrophe.

As shown in an earlier example, the person whose car wouldn't start overreacted by thinking it would be necessary to buy a whole new vehicle, rather than just a new battery. In that case, a somewhat small problem was blown way out of proportion and viewed as a catastrophe.

Your mind clings to worst-case scenarios, such as, "My son did not get into a good enough college; now he'll never be successful."

Examples

Here are a few other examples.

My boss texted me to schedule a call. We never meet unless something is wrong. I'm probably going to be reprimanded for some offense. I'm dreading that call.

I really blew that presentation yesterday. The boss didn't really want to promote me to account executive. I'm probably going to get fired.

It's 1:00 in the morning and my son is not home yet. He said he'd text if he were going to be late. He's not responding to my calls or texts. I'm so worried he's been in an accident. I won't be able to get to sleep until he gets home.

After a disagreement with someone, have you ever thought to yourself, *"That guy, Sam is such a bully."*

Have you ever entered your favorite coffee shop with maybe three people in line, only to think to yourself, *"OMG, the line is so long today. It drives me crazy when the line is so long."*

Have you ever had to wait on hold for customer service, only to be connected to someone who cannot really solve your problem?

You can see how relatively small problems can be blown out of proportion and viewed as a catastrophe.

More Examples

Here are some over-reactions that may sound familiar.

It drives me crazy (or stresses me out) when...

- It drives me crazy when I have to wait on hold for tech support.
- It drives me crazy when there is a lot of traffic.
- It drives me crazy when my co-worker does not pull his own weight.
- It drives me crazy when I can't get my work finished because I have too much.
- It drives me crazy when my project manager is disorganized or micro-manages my work.

Think about how you react in the following circumstances:

- *When someone at home or work criticizes something I do, I...*
- *When someone cuts me off in traffic, I ...*
- *When a customer service person either does not know how to handle a problem or gives me an answer I do not find satisfactory, I ...*

- *When someone gives me wrong directions, I ...*
- *When the service in a store or restaurant is poor, I...*
- *When my boss does not acknowledge my hard work, I feel...*
- *When I give a suggestion in a meeting & my answer is ignored or shot down, I feel ....*

In what ways do you tend to over-react or exaggerate a situation?

Exercise

What drives you crazy or stresses you out? Use either some of the examples above or insert your own.

_____

_____

_____

_____

_____

Reality Spin

Now let's look at how you could mitigate your reaction to the annoyances or situations that come up in your life.

For example, traffic is annoying for everybody, but you choose how to react. So, being prepared for heavy traffic can go a long way to maintaining a positive attitude. For example, the **reality spin** would be to decide in advance you are not going to let the traffic upset you. You support that plan by choosing to tune in to some relaxing classical music or having a fun comedy podcast or interesting audio book ready to go. That way you can keep your mind off the annoying traffic. Why let traffic ruin your mood?

> # You can change your reactions by changing your irrational thinking.

Another example is from one of the situations above in which the worker did a bad job on her presentation & is fearful of getting fired. The **reality spin** would sound something like this: "I'm not usually such a bad presenter. I should have gotten a better night's sleep. It was an isolated incident. It's unreasonable to expect to get fired. Next time I can practice more and get a friend to critique me."

Putting a **Reality Spin** on an over-reaction or exaggeration is especially helpful because it gives you control and much-needed perspective for developing healthier responses to stress. The examples below illustrate this type of distorted stress response, along with suggestions for reframing overreactions and exaggerations with a **Reality Spin**.

Over-Reaction / Exaggeration	*Reality Spin*
I wasn't able to complete the quarterly report today. That's it! I know I'm going to lose my job!	*Perhaps I can get an extension on the deadline. I can talk to my supervisor about the report and/or get additional help to complete it. Maybe I need to talk to him about restructuring my duties and/or deadlines. Since I've gotten good reviews, I don't really expect I'll get fired over this one issue.*
We cannot find the Power Point for my manager's presentation tomorrow. This is a disaster! My head is on the chopping block!	*Perhaps I can work together with my manager or co-worker to re-create the PowerPoint. Perhaps someone else in the office has a backup copy or knows where it is. I can enlist support from the IT department to search the server data files.*

Exercise

What are some coping mechanisms you can use for the situations that stress you out?

List some of your over-reactions and exaggerations and then work to counter the reactions with a rational **Reality Spin**.

Over-Reaction / Exaggeration	*Reality Spin*

Recognize Over-Generalization

Another common reaction when we get upset is to over-generalize. That means to take an occurrence and generalize it to become something that *always* happens, or by contrast, to claim that it *never* does. Also pay attention to the words *every* and *all*, that get sprinkled into our conversations when we over-generalize. See if any of the examples of over-generalizations below resonate with you. Then look at how a **Reality Spin** could be applied in each situation.

Examples

Over-Generalization	Reality Spin
He is **always** late.	*Is he **always** late? Or does it just seem that way because it's so annoying when you are waiting for someone and this kind of thing happens more often than you'd like. Is it really **always**?*
***Every** time I write emails to my users or customers, my manager criticizes me.*	*Does your manager actually criticize your emails **every** time you write one? Or could it be because, when she gets pressure from a senior manager over emails, she is extra irritable?*
*The software manager **never** gives me any feedback or attention.*	*Is it true that the software manager **never** gives you attention? Or, does it just seem that way because she is really busy and does not have time to stop and chat?*

Over-Generalization	Reality Spin
All of my office mates are always talking so loudly.	Are **all** of your office mates loud talkers? Could your office have bad acoustics that make some voices seem louder? Or do you get distracted by conversations when you are under pressure to finish a project? Could you move to a quieter space within your building?
My work friend, Jodi, is **always** criticizing me **every** time I see her.	Is it true that Jodi **always** criticizes you **every** time you talk to her? Or does it just feel that way because when she does, she uses a harsh tone of voice?

Do you see how we often blow situations out of proportion by over-generalizing?

Over-generalizing causes us to lose perspective.

Exercise

What are some of your over-generalizations about various stressful situations or incidents, and how could you apply the **Reality Spin**, based on rational, honest assessment of the stressor?

Over-Generalization	Reality Spin

Combat Stressful "Shoulds"

Use of the word "should" when thinking about yourself is a flag that you are engaging in a form of self-criticism. This self-criticism triggers negative feelings that cause stress. Using the word "should" is another way of saying "I am not good enough." You are good enough; you just may want to set a goal for yourself. There's nothing wrong with self-improvement, but the wording, even to yourself, is critical.

A "should" statement indicates an expectation you have of yourself or some situation in your life. That expectation is that you need to be different in some way, better than you already are.

Instead of "should" try using a "preference" statement. For example, rather than, "I should be able to save more money," how about "I'd like to learn how to save more money. I am going to set a goal to learn about money via a book, financial wellness class offered at work, or a financial advisor."

Combatting stressful "shoulds" in your life begins with identifying your expectations and then replacing them with preferences and goals, when appropriate.

Examples

Do you find yourself saying or thinking "should" statements like the ones below?

- *I should be able to handle that problem more easily.*
- *I should be better at managing my time.*
- *I should be able to save more money.*
- *I should exercise more.*
- *I should be more organized.*
- *I should get my work done without having to stay late at the office so often.*

Once you have identified a "should" statement that you commonly make, the next step is to replace the "should" statement with a *preference* and, when appropriate, a *goal*.

Let's look at how this works using one of the statements from above:

Should: I **should** exercise more.

Preference: I would prefer it if I could exercise at least three times per week.

Goal: I am going to put my favorite exercise on my calendar and put my workout clothes in my car, so I can go straight to my favorite hiking location on my way home from work.

Or… I am going to download an exercise app, so that I can work out before or after work or during my lunch break.

Or… I am going to check with one of my co-workers to see if anyone wants to join me for some outdoor activity, like a walk once a week.

Examples

Now here are a few other examples to give you more ideas about how to combat stressful "should" statements.

Should: I **should** be able to get to work on time.

Preference: I would prefer it if I could get to work on time more often. I could try going to bed ten minutes earlier.

Goal: For the next seven days I will go to bed ten minutes earlier and set my alarm to wake me ten minutes earlier.

Should: I **should** be able to get my work done in eight hours.

Preference: I would prefer it if I could manage my time. I'm going to set this as a goal.

Goal: Write out a daily schedule.

Exercise

What are your *should's*? Make a list here.

_____

_____

_____

_____

_____

Which is/are the most important *should(s)* to you?

_____

_____

_____

The next step is to convert your should statement into a preference statement with a possible goal attached, when appropriate.

Preference: I would prefer it if I could…

_____

_____

_____

_____

Goal: I am going to (take specific action that is a fit for your life) …

_____

_____

_____

_____

On (specific day and time)….

_____

How did that feel?

_____

_____

_____

_____

Know Your Stress / Spin Your Stress

Tool #3:
Unpack Your Emotional Baggage

Photo by Frank Sonnenberg Online on Unsplash. Used under Standard License.

One thing I learned from my studies of psychology, my experience working in the IT department at three companies, my 20 years as a technology recruiter, and my work on my own emotional health is that many people come to work with their own set of "baggage," so to speak. In case you are not familiar with this expression, carrying "emotional baggage" refers to carrying a load of old hurts, insecurities, wounds, or other feelings that have not been resolved, usually from childhood. When people hold on to these emotional burdens, it can intensely impact the way they behave and respond to stress in the current day.

Consider this example from a client. We'll call her Amrita. A family member used to make a comment that might sound perfectly ordinary to someone from any other family. "You need to be at my house tonight by 6:00." But every time Amrita was asked to do something that started with, "You need to..." she would get upset and feel knots in her stomach. Amrita came to me frustrated and confused by her reaction. Together we dug deeper to figure out what was really going on. It was her vehement over-reaction that clued me into the fact that something deeper was bothering her. After careful analysis and working with the tools in this workbook, Amrita and I realized that when she heard the words "you need to…" she interpreted it as a demand, which reminded her of all the extreme demands her parents used to place on her.

When Amrita recognized how hearing the words "you need to" sent her unconscious stress response into overdrive, she was able to apply the **Reality Spin** technique. That enabled her to change her reaction, feel calmer and more capable of responding in an appropriate manner to requests instead of getting tangled up in her old emotional baggage.

When you *unpack your emotional baggage*, you clear out the cobwebs of your memories and learn that a current situation has nothing to do with your past. More importantly you become aware of situations where you may be over-reacting to something in your current life that triggers an unresolved emotion or situation from your past. Any time you catch yourself in an over-reaction, ask yourself, "does this situation really warrant this extreme a reaction? What else may be causing me to act this way?"

Another example is when you take things very personally, such as when someone criticizes you, talks down to you, or you mistakenly take a comment as a criticism and get very upset. It is worth repeating that any time you get very upset or over-react to anything someone says or does, that is a sure sign that you are reacting to a hidden childhood tangle that is still plaguing you today.

Dr. Elayne Savage explains in her book *Don't Take It Personally! The Art of Dealing with Rejection* that childhood rejection wounds come from parents, teachers, siblings, extended family, and friends. Rejection and criticism become internalized and develop into self-limiting beliefs in adulthood. These beliefs are what stop us from reaching for our highest goals and desires in life and also stop us from asking for what we want or need at work. These might include confronting difficult challenges, asking for a promotion or raise or taking certain actions, like speaking to an executive, cold calling on sales prospects, or volunteering to make presentations. It's sort of like knowing not to touch a hot iron because you know you will get burned. The same is true of the neural pathways, or thought patterns, discussed in **Tool #2**.

Savage goes on to explain that we all rightly wanted love and respect growing up. When we did not get them, we didn't fully actualize to become our best self, a thriving, happy adult, who knows how to ask for what she wants and does not take everything personally. For example, one client recounted often coming home as a child, with a 93 on a tough exam, only to be chastised for missing the other 7 points. As a result, she stopped trying to get respect from her parents.

These types of rejection messages get translated to "you're not good enough" or "you're not smart enough". To make matters worse, we internalize the messages and develop a bad habit of telling ourselves the same negative messages into our adult life. These negative tapes create a lack of trust in other people and impact the way we see our world and ourselves. They also impact our sense of psychological safety.

Often we are not even aware of these early hurts lying dormant. They sometimes crop up and cause us to feel wounded in our adult life, often without realizing we are over-reacting, exaggerating, or over-generalizing, the patterns discussed in **Tool #2**. As you can see, an early abundance of rejection and criticism is the genesis of these patterns that stop us from living an emotionally healthy life.

Often, we run on *automatic,* so to speak. We don't even realize what is causing us to act the way we do. Have you ever heard someone say, "that's just the way I am"? In reality, those automatic patterns come from childhood or other early incidents.

When you focus on understanding the origins of your childhood patterns that are plaguing you today, you will begin to change your behavior.

While it is important to uncover the repressed hurtful experiences that can hinder your professional progress, **Tool #3** is not a replacement for psychotherapy. But using this tool to unpack your emotional baggage will help you strengthen your ability to *move from stress to success.*

The steps in **Tool #3** are similar to others in this workbook in that you'll start by building awareness and then you'll use that awareness to change your outlook and behavior. To begin, you will look back at your early life to identify where your irrational stress responses may have originated. Then you will do an exercise to unpack your emotional baggage so that you can move forward feeling lighter and more confident.

Identify the Source of Your Stress Responses

Consider the following stories.

Sarah: Sarah's co-worker Karen, whom she liked, asked to borrow the Power Point slides she had spent weeks developing. Sarah snapped back with an angry "No!" and walked away feeling resentful.

Gene: Gene's manager made a casual comment about a few grammatical errors in a report he had written. Gene suddenly felt knots in his stomach, to the point where he had to excuse himself. He headed to the restroom to be out of earshot from others and quietly grumbled about being treated unfairly.

In each of these scenarios, the responses were excessive, given the circumstances. And the source for these distorted responses stemmed from childhood experiences. Sarah had a younger sister who constantly borrowed her belongings, with their mother's permission, and hardly ever returned any of them, or left her clothing crumpled and dirty on the floor of their shared bedroom. And, Gene's parents were extremely critical and demanding about his schoolwork and berated him for the tiniest mistakes.

Once Sarah and Gene had a chance to identify the trigger for their overreactions, they were more equipped to understand that they were over-reacting, based on emotional tangles from their past. Then based on that understanding, they could live a healthier emotional life.

Here is a basic tip to help you identify where your own distorted stress responses may originate:

Any time you get extremely upset or over-react to something someone else says or does, that is a sign that you could be reacting to a hidden tangle from childhood, that is still plaguing you today.

Example

Ying Yue: A more complex case is that of Ying Yue. Every time Ying Yue got critiqued or criticized for some aspect of her work, whether constructively or not, she took it very personally. Yes, criticism can hurt, but how much upset is rational and for what length of time? Ying Yue would feel very hurt and let the feelings bother her for several days. It got to the point that she felt nervous every time her boss called her into her office.

Eventually, with the help of the **Stress Audit** from **Tool #1,** combined with the exercises below**,** she realized that she was repeating a pattern that stemmed from her childhood. I advised her to think back to her childhood to connect to a time when she was criticized, so that she could figure out why she got so upset and let it go on for so long. It turned out that every time her mother criticized her, she made fun of and chastised her in front of the whole family and continued to tease her for several days. It's no wonder that Ying Yue did not react well to criticism. This realization was a powerful awakening for Ying Yue, and she was able to put her present interactions with her boss into context and to realize that her boss was not treating her the same way her mother did, and that she was just trying to help her improve at work.

Now when Ying Yue is criticized, she immediately writes down how she feels. She is able to lessen the sting, if there is any, and let it go much sooner.

Can you see how powerful it is to unpack your emotional baggage to help you heal the wounds still lingering from your childhood?

Exercise

This exercise offers you an opportunity to begin unpacking your emotional baggage and untangling your hurts and triggers from childhood experiences, so that they do not continue to plague you today. Set aside some quiet time to consider and then answer the questions that follow.

First, think back to a situation in the recent past when you felt excessively upset or out of sorts. Perhaps you realized you over-reacted or responded to an incident in a way that is out of character for you. Maybe someone criticized the way you performed a task or disagreed with something you suggested in a rude tone of voice. Or worse, perhaps someone harshly disagreed with you in front of others, cutting you down in the process. Perhaps you did not do something you were supposed to do at work, or perhaps you did something wrong. For this part of the exercise, you are only pinpointing a recent incident when you felt hurt or upset.

What happened? How did you feel?

(Note: You may want to refer to the **Stress Audit**, from **Tool #1** for this question.)

_____

_____

_____

_____

_____

_____

_____

Now, try to recall a childhood or other previous experience that this stressful incident triggered for you? Can you link this incident or situation, or simply your feelings about it to a specific event or pattern from your childhood? If so, describe that event and how you felt. Be specific about the people involved, how old you were, and where you were. What were the other people saying to you?

These additional questions may help you remember a particular event or experience:

- What is the similar feeling or connection between the deep pang of hurt, anger, or resentment you are experiencing today, and what happened in your past?
- When in your childhood were you made to feel bad about yourself? Was one or both of your parents overly critical or did they have unreasonable expectations of you in everything that you did?
- Are you still trying to live up to those unreasonable expectations?
- Or did some other trauma happen in your childhood that left a deep wound for you, that bleeds every time you have a difficult conflict?
- Are you still trying to get the attention one or both parents were never able to give you?

Even if you don't have memories of a negative childhood experience, are you holding on to something else that happened in your early life or since you started working, that could be the source of your current extreme stress reactions?

_____

_____

_____

_____

_____

_____

_____

_____

_____

_____

Are you beginning to see how your early childhood patterns or other inciting incidents are at the root of your emotional life today?

_____

_____

_____

_____

_____

_____

_____

_____

Unpack Your Bags

Once you start examining your past, you will begin to see how your intense stress responses are rooted in earlier patterns of behavior, the genesis of your emotional triggers.

Photo by sabthai on DepositPhotos.com. Used under Standard License.

Identifying the origin of a particular distorted stress response, as you did in the preceding exercise, is the first step in dis-entangling your past experiences from your present behavior. After that, you can apply the **Reality Spin** technique to your responses to unleash your old, extreme reactions and let them go.

Examples

In the box below, you'll see some ways a **Reality Spin** can be applied to the earlier memories and stressful incidents experienced in the cases of Sarah, Gene, and Ying Yue described in the previous section.

Keep in mind that sometimes it takes time and focus to find the connecting trigger from the past. It's not always obvious, but whatever idea pops into your mind is usually the best place to begin.

Current Stress + Past Memory	Reality Spin
Sarah: I can't believe Karen wants to borrow my Power Point slides after I worked so hard on them. She reminds me of my sister, taking my things. I hope I never have to work with Karen again!	Karen reminds me of Sister, and all the times she borrowed anything she wanted, any time she wanted. It made me so angry then, especially because Mother seemed to take her side. In reality Karen is usually a supportive co-worker, and we've gotten along well on other projects. I have to remind myself that she's not my sister, and the boss is not my mother. Karen is not out to steal anything. I'll apologize for snapping at her and talk with her to come up with a reasonable plan for sharing our work.
Gene: It seems like I can't do anything right. Why does my manager have to pick on the smallest mistakes I make instead of seeing everything else I did right? My parents were the same way. It's totally unfair!	I know my manager is really trying to give me helpful feedback. Yes, my parents were overly critical and demanding, but that was then, and this is now. It's okay for me to make mistakes. I can learn from them. No one is completely perfect and that includes me. My boss is only trying to help me succeed at work.
Ying Yue: I'm getting criticized again by the boss. It's so frustrating that she is always finding something to criticize. She is so mean. Every time she calls me into her office, my heart starts pounding. I don't like interacting with her.	This situation reminds me of all the times Mother would tease me for making mistakes. I was just a young girl then. There is really no way that my manager is treating me the same way Mother did. She is not always criticizing me. She does not embarrass me in front of the group, and she is not overly critical. She is simply trying to help me perform better. Now, I realize that she has my best interests at heart and is trying to help me grow my career.

Do you see how taking the time to make an honest assessment of a situation can help you take the reality spin approach and not wallow in your old emotional patterns?

It's not only your childhood...

While early life clearly has a deep and significant impact on all aspects of human development and behavior, childhood experiences may not be the only source of your distorted stress responses.

Consider what happened to Mike. He felt blindsided when his boss suddenly pulled the plug on a project that Mike had shepherded through many ups and downs. Mike eventually left that company. But when he started his new position, he was defensive and uncooperative when offered the chance to head another project team. Because he had not unpacked his emotional baggage from the previous job, he carried it with him into the new one. Might you still be carrying old baggage from previous jobs or situations?

Exercise

In the previous section you wrote about a situation in the current day that caused you extreme pain. You even uncovered the genesis of that pain by connecting it to a situation from your earlier life.

Now the next step is to put the **Reality Spin** on that situation and your reaction. Ask yourself if the criticism or pain you experienced from the recent event really warranted the level of hurt or emotion you felt. Or were you projecting the pain from your early life onto the current day?

Then apply the **Reality Spin** to your thoughts and feelings about the incident or situation, to reframe that reaction using rational logic and facts, in order to develop a more appropriate response, as you saw in the examples above.

_____

_____

_____

_____

_____

_____

_____

_____

_____

_____

_____

This next exercise is one of the most powerful in your toolkit. Imagine you are an older, wiser, more rational version of yourself who has overcome all of your emotional baggage. Write out what your wise self would tell your hurt child still experiencing emotional pain, to explain how and why the early life experience is not a parallel to the current day, and how it really is okay to let go of all that pain and pressure. You might remind your hurt child that your parents may not have realized all the pain they were causing, and that deep down they probably wanted only the best for you.

_____

_____

_____

_____

_____

_____

_____

_____

_____

_____

_____

_____

_____

_____

_____

_____

_____

_____

_____

_____

_____

_____

What did you learn from that conversation with your wiser self?

_____

_____

_____

_____

_____

_____

_____

Before we close out this important tool, I want you to think about forgiveness. Now that you have reignited those painful childhood memories, it is important to remember that your parents and teachers did the best they could. It is okay to forgive them for the ills they bestowed upon you because forgiveness is for you, the forgiver. And, forgiveness helps you to let go of the past and evolve into the person you wish to be.

I know it seems a little odd for me to tell you to go deep to bring up the past and then I tell you to let go of it. You do need to take the time to process it, for sure. But you don't want to let those wounds stop you from becoming your best self today.

Unpack Your Bags

Tool #4:
Practice Self-Care

Now that you have dug deep to uncover and hopefully begin to heal some old emotional wounds, we are going to come back to the surface and talk about physical and mental stress. While there is nothing that can match the difficult work you did in **Tool #3**, physical and mental self-care are other critical parts of managing your stress.

Physical self-care includes healthy nutrition, regular physical activity, and adequate sleep. Of course, each aspect of self-care impacts the others, meaning when you are sleep-deprived you don't have the energy to exercise or think critically at work. When you don't eat healthfully, you sometimes feel negative about yourself and are not motivated to exercise. So, practicing self-care helps you develop a healthy body and a positive mind, which will enable you to be more resilient and resourceful when facing stressful situations.

Eat Well

What you put in your body can affect your mood.

You probably already know that eating a well-balanced diet is critical for health. What you put in your body can affect your mood. There are countless eating plans available in books or on the internet. Government guidelines are easily found online, such as the USDA *Choose My Plate* Plan or the *DASH* Diet (*Dietary Approaches to Stop Hypertension*).

Whichever plan you choose, it's advisable to get enough of a balance of nutrients, which come from the following: vegetables, fruit, whole grains, legumes, healthy fats, and protein (from whatever source you prefer). Of course, you have to make the right choice that works for you.

Some people have to eat multiple small meals each day, and others do better eating three main meals with one or two light snacks. You may have to experiment a bit to find the eating style that best fits because there are many ways to eat healthfully. If you are unsure what and how to eat, I recommend seeking the advice of a registered dietitian or other professional.

When we are stressed or life gets hectic, we tend to grab any convenient food because we don't think we have the time to prepare healthy meals or snacks. That kind of eating can lead us to over-indulge, which clouds the thinking and makes it harder to resist extreme stress responses.

Healthy food preparation does not have to take a lot of time. When you go grocery shopping, make sure to buy enough of everything you need for the week, and then prepare little "grab 'n go" baggies of cut-up vegetables and other healthy snacks. Alternatively, you can buy pre-packaged snacks. Healthy eating does not have to be complicated or time-consuming, and it's an important part of a healthy body and happy mind, both of which help you avoid the kind of stress responses that lead to burnout.

One habit that is easy to fall into at work is choosing high salt or high sugar snacks with a dose of caffeine in the afternoon, when our energy tends to wane. After the effect of these stimulants wears off, we are more susceptible to stress.

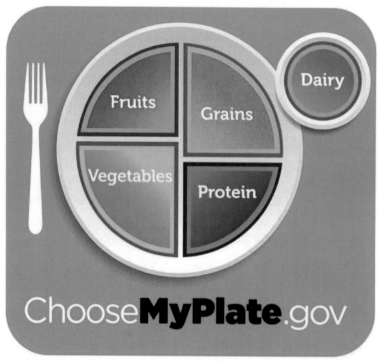

Image by <u>USDA's Center for Nutrition Policy and Promotion</u>. *Used under standard license.*

You probably don't even realize how many calories or grams of sugar are inside those "fun coffee drinks" you like. Most coffee shops maintain a binder of nutrition facts for their specialty drinks.

Instead of drinking another cup of coffee in the afternoon, try taking a short walk outside. This can counter the desire for caffeine. The physical activity gets the blood pumping and releases endorphins, the feel-good hormone. Furthermore, another positive by-product of getting active outdoors is enhanced clarity and problem-solving.

Another problem is that in some high-paced workplaces, people get so busy during the day that they work though lunch and get so light-headed in the afternoon that they can't think straight. Then they grab a quick, unhealthy snack like a caffeinated drink and sugary bar. So healthy eating also involves getting enough of the proper nutrition.

Drinking plenty of water is another important part of nutrition so you don't get dehydrated, a condition, which also stymies productivity at work.

As you've learned from the other tools, building awareness is the first step towards behavior change. If you're already eating well, acknowledge it and move on to the next section.

If you think your eating habits need improvement, you may want to keep a food diary, or you might monitor your intake of certain foods or beverages, like desserts, unhealthy snacks, or high calorie drinks. There are free apps that make food tracking easy.

One idea is to simply make the decision to focus on one small improvement, such as focusing on healthy snacks in the afternoon or whenever you are most apt to eat unhealthy foods.

Another plan to move you closer to healthier eating is to start out by making the healthy food choice one day a week. Mondays are the best day because you are freshest the first day of the work week.

Examples

I am having coffee drinks with sugary syrup every day. I am going to either bask for sugar-free syrup or cut out those drinks twice a week.

I eat unhealthy snacks every afternoon. I am going to eat something healthy like fruit and then decide if I'm still hungry.

I often order French fries at lunch, so I'm going to order a salad at least once a week.

I rarely drink water, mostly sodas. I am going to start by drinking at least one glass of water every day.

Tip

Read labels. Did you know how much sugar is in everyday foods like ketchup, salad dressing, and tomato sauce, not to mention coke and apple juice, and even yogurts pre-packaged with fruit.

Exercise

Write one thing you will do to improve your eating habits, whether it's simply building awareness, eliminating a particular food, cutting back on that food, or adopting a new food plan. Once you've taken that first step, you can return to this exercise and build by adding new healthy habits.

To improve my nutrition, I will:

_____

_____

_____

_____

_____

Engage in Regular Physical Activity

Physical activity is a known stress-reliever. That is because endorphins, one of the happiness chemicals, are released in the brain when you work out aerobically at a moderate or high intensity level.

Did you know that both the U.S. Surgeon General and the American Heart Association recommend 150 minutes per week of moderate intensity activity, or 75 minutes per week of high intensity, for optimal health? Basically, they suggest you move every day.

Here is my formula for making fitness fun and as a consequence, intrinsically motivating, which means truly satisfying and sustainable:

- **Fun:** It has to be fun or you won't keep it up. Do you like to play volleyball, tennis, golf, bowl or dance? Choose an activity you really enjoy.
- **Social Element:** Either invite a friend or family member or find a group fitness class being taught via Zoom, or at a community center. Social outings release oxytocin, a happiness chemical, so they add to the enjoyment and mutual support.
- **Regular schedule:** Choose a specific time and day that will work for your life. That is how to develop a new habit.

Physical activity is a known stress-reliever.

Photo by Rawpixel on DepositPhotos.com. Used under Standard License.

Another way to increase your physical activity level is by simply moving more throughout the day. This form of activity is referred to as **NEAT**, or **Non-Exercise Activity Thermogenesis**.

Examples

Here are a number of ways to practice NEAT activities on a daily basis:

- Park far from the entrance to buildings
- Take the stairs instead of elevators or escalators
- Take five-minute walking breaks around the office, especially when you need to speak to a co-worker, rather than emailing or texting
- Walk while meeting
- Walk around the mall or a park
- Alternate sitting and standing at your desk. Consider a treadmill desk.
- Stand or walk in place when talking on the phone
- Stand when in a Zoom meeting
- Garden
- Dance at home
- Clean to music
- Consider a stationary bike at your home office.

Exercise

Every move you make counts. If you are not already physically active, what ideas do you have for choosing a physical activity or simply moving more throughout the day?

_____

_____

_____

_____

_____

_____

In order to set a new physical activity goal, try the following statement.

To take care of myself today, I will (state physical activity) _____

_____

at (exact time or as needed) _____

In order to be prepared, I will _____

_____

To make fitness fun and keep me committed, I will invite _____ *to join me.*

Get Adequate Sleep

Sleep quality and quantity have a huge impact on your mood and productivity during working hours. Sleep insufficiency, insomnia, and other untreated sleep disorders are a growing concern for the American workforce, and you may be among those workers struggling with sleep issues.

Adults need between seven and eight hours of sleep each night for optimum health.

Photo by monkeybusiness *on* DepositPhotos.com. *Used under Standard License.*

The purpose of sleep is to rest and recharge to bring the body back to homeostasis. Important bodily functions such as repair and rejuvenation occur during sleep, including making new blood cells, memory processing, healing, and even brain cleansing.[1]

In *The Sleep Revolution: Transforming Your Life, One Night at a Time,* Ariana Huffington points out that "sleep has a profound effect on the brain's Prefrontal Cortex, home of advanced cognitive processes, such as planning, decision-making, and problem solving." Further, sleep gives us strength, energy, power, and creativity, and makes us happier, less anxious, more productive, and more able to handle daily stress.

Of course, stress can also have an impact on the quality of your sleep. It is important to develop good nighttime habits that minimize stress and calm you to transition to peaceful sleep.

When you don't get a good night's sleep, you can experience a depressed immune system, lapse of attention, slow thinking, irritability, poor memory, poor judgment, anxiety, depression, increased accidents, decreased productivity, lack of focus, and difficulty interacting with other team members at work. Sufficient sleep is integral to the way you function during your waking hours.

Fundamentally, stress impacts sleep and sleep impacts stress, so it's important to try to practice good sleep hygiene. Below you'll see a few examples of ways to address sleep issues.

> ## Stress impacts sleep, and sleep impacts stress.

Examples

If you have problems sleeping, Nancy H. Rothstein, **The Sleep Ambassador®**[2] recommends having a nightly sleep routine, that may include the following:

- Take a warm shower or bath
- Enjoy a cup of sleep-friendly tea (caffeine-free or herbal)
- Read a relaxing book
- Ensure the temperature in your bedroom is conducive for sleep (65 – 68 degrees)
- Maintain a consistent bed and wake time to support your circadian rhythm
- Put your phone away about an hour before you go to sleep

Exercise

If you are suffering from sleep issues write down at least three steps you will take starting tonight to improve your sleep hygiene.

_____

_____

_____

Go Outside

Did you know that scientists claim that spending time outdoors helps you relax and clear your mind, in addition to giving you benefits from Vitamin D? Also, the light from sunshine helps you regulate your sleep. "Sunlight improves the communication between the regions of the brain that are central to our handling of emotions such as stress and anxiety," says PhD fellow Brenda McMahon, MD, of the Neurobiology Research Unit at the Copenhagen University Hospital, Denmark.[1]

Photo by SimpleFoto on DepositPhotos.com. Used under standard license.

Sunlight relieves stress by lowering cortisol, the stress hormone.[2] Additionally, sunlight causes our brains to produce serotonin[3], a happiness hormone that can improve mood by alleviating pain, providing energy and making us feel happy and well-rested. Sunlight also produces endorphins[4], mentioned earlier and known as the "feel-good hormone."

Melatonin is a hormone that regulates sleep and makes us tired. Sunlight slows down our body's ability to make it. That's why we're naturally awake during the day and sleepy at night. Allow yourself to sync up with nature's clock in order to set a steady circadian rhythm for yourself. By getting enough natural light, your body's inner clock will get on track, giving you a better night's sleep and more energy during the day, plus making you more resilient in the face of stress.

Furthermore, research indicates that when we feel weary around 3:00 pm taking a short walk outdoors boosts concentration and productivity, alleviating the need for that afternoon cup of coffee.[5]

In summary, spending time outdoors everyday helps to reduce stress, enhance happiness, improve clarity, and regulate sleep. What an easy way to fill yourself up with good feelings.

Examples

Here are a few suggestions for increasing your time outdoors:

- Take a walk at lunch time or around 3 p.m. to boost concentration and productivity
- Open windows and take in deep breaths of fresh air – even for a few minutes each day.
- Find new activities or hobbies with built-in reasons for going outside, such as playing tennis, birdwatching, or hiking. Or consider getting a dog that requires daily walks.
- Consider riding your bike to run nearby errands.

Exercise

List at least three ways you can incorporate more time outdoors in your daily life.

_____

_____

_____

_____

_____

_____

Hold a Morning Perspective Meeting

Now that we've discussed physical self-care let's dive into mental self-care. Managing your daily perspective is one of those mental self-care activities that can be accomplished with a morning ritual known as *Morning Pages*. This idea comes from a book called *The Artist's Way* by Julia Cameron. The book was originally intended for artists and writers, but it applies to anyone who would like to connect to themselves.

The book suggests committing to writing only three pages per day longhand when you first awaken. Often what happens is that you write more, but it feels like a daunting task to commit to writing ten pages. So you commit to only three. The main function of *Morning Pages* is to act as a *brain drain*. That is, it allows you to clear your brain of thoughts and feelings before starting your day. The writing doesn't have to be anything fancy or elaborate. There is no right or wrong way to do morning writing. Daniel Pink, author of *Drive: The Surprising Truth About What Motivates Us* tells us that sometimes you don't know what you think until you start writing. That is the beauty of writing.

Photo by The Creative Exchange on Unsplash. Used under Standard License.

If three pages sounds like too much, you can always cut down the assignment by jotting down a few thoughts on your phone, to clear your head before you get caught up in your day's activities.

Exercise

One way to begin your morning writing ritual is to start with the following prompt:

Today I feel _____ *and need* _____.

The point is to let go of any residual negativity from the previous day and not to fill your mind with worry over the day to come. Writing down your feelings helps to clear the worry out of your consciousness and bring up issues you didn't even know were there lying dormant. You may want to use a separate notebook for these pages and review them in your Morning Perspective Meeting with yourself. Having a notebook will also enable you to keep a log and note your stress response patterns along with how you're dealing with stressors in your life.

Today I feel
_____

_____

_____

_____

_____

_____

_____

and need
_____

_____

_____

_____

_____

_____

_____

Practice Self-Care

Tool #5:
Set Healthy Boundaries

Not saying *no,* but wishing you had can cause frustration and stress for many of you. This behavior pattern happens when you have not been taught how to say *no* or have not seen effective role models demonstrate how to say *no.* Saying *no* is simply a skill that is easy to learn.

Like all new skills, it just takes practice.

Of course, in the workplace you may feel you are supposed to say *yes* to any request that comes from your boss or one of the leaders. But where do you draw the line?

Photo by motortion via stock.adobe.com. Used under Standard License.

In this tool you will learn how to set healthy boundaries by identifying the feeling of overwhelm, communicating your needs, asking for feedback, and saying *no* at work, at home, and to yourself. And then, finally you will learn how to manage your projects and plan your time.

First, it is important to note that there are many untrained or unprepared managers in the workplace who were promoted for technical skills, not emotional intelligence or project management skills.

In that case you may need to manage your own workload and "manage up." That means being strategic about helping your boss and team with projects, and more importantly, communicating your needs after getting to know them. Daniel Pink, author of When: The Scientific Secrets of Perfect Timing advises when managing up to keep in mind, *what's in it for the manager*?

It has been widely documented that people leave bosses not companies. What part can you play in developing a good relationship with your boss?

One of the key facets of a strong relationship is trust, and trust is built by spending time together. If your boss does not invite you, then you can invite him or her to coffee, just to "get to know each other better," or "understand the goals for the team."

I realize this won't work in every situation, but when appropriate, give it a try. If you feel hesitant, you could say you just want to make sure you are tracking properly with all of your projects because you want to perform well. Just ask for 10 or 15 minutes. It will likely expand into 30. If the manager has not articulated his mission for the team, ask him. This time well spent will create goodwill and will help you understand what makes your manager tick and vice versa.

Find common ground by studying her Linkedin profile before you meet. At some point, you will want to ask for something or need to push back on an issue. The trust you are developing now will strengthen your position for the future.

Try to end every encounter on a positive note that lingers, so that the next meeting begins with that positive tone.

Any time you bring a problem to the boss, try to bring a constructive solution, as well and try to make that solution a *win:win*.

Identify Burnout and Set Limits at Work

Do you recognize the warning signs when you begin to feel overwhelmed by too many responsibilities and demands? Do you push ahead no matter what?

Sometimes, it's hard to admit that you've reached your limit and need to take a break. Maybe you frantically do more and more in an attempt to keep up, until a big mistake brings your efforts screeching to a halt. Or perhaps you stop only when you get sick. Or maybe you just give up.

Photo by alphaspirit via stock.adobe.com. Used under Standard License.

Here are a few signals that your workload may be causing you to feel the beginnings of burnout:

- Mental or physical exhaustion
- Feelings of ineffectiveness
- Disengagement or isolation
- Higher sensitivity to feedback
- Avoidance of everyday situations, especially your least favorite work tasks
- Snapping at co-workers, customers, or family members
- Sleep problems
- Digestive issues
- Engaging in angry outbursts
- Feeling resentful

Each of these negative signals is a symptom of extreme stress. Rather than waiting until things are boiling over, practice noticing when you are beginning to feel overwhelmed at work or at home. Jot these feelings down in your *Morning Pages* described in the previous section. Then communicate what's happening to your manager or at least to your accountability partner or mentor. Remember, no one knows how you feel if you do not tell them, especially your manager. They can't read your mind.

Now that you realize you are reaching your limits it is time to set boundaries with your manager. When communicating that you are feeling overwhelmed, or on the verge of it, it's important to stay calm and speak rationally. That is the best way to engage your manager. Also, consider, when appropriate, demonstrating your case with specific evidence, such as time needed to complete a project compared to how many days remain before the deadline.

According to the book, *Ask For It*, by Linda Babcock and Sara Laschever, many people, especially women try to make the best of things and do not ask for what they need. As discussed in **Tool #3** not asking for what you need is caused by one of those self-limiting beliefs developed from early rejection and criticism. Remember there are things in life we can control and things we can't. You may not be able to control everything about your work, but you can certainly ask for what you need.

Communicating that a project is out of control is not really saying *no,* but rather letting your manager know that the workload is out of balance. So setting boundaries is sometimes about knowing when and how to communicate the status of a project. You are not really saying *no* to your boss, you are simply communicating that the situation needs attention.

Examples

There's a problem we need to solve. My current workload constitutes over 40 hours of work. I am a team player, but I am exhausted from working overtime, and I need to be at home at a reasonable time. Is there someone who can take some of the less technical parts of the project? Or can the deadline be amended?

Of course, this statement assumes you are organized with your time. If you aren't, you will find the **Manage Your Projects: Plan Your Time** section at the end of this Tool helpful.

Another common circumstance is the case when the boss comes to you with an "exciting new project." As wonderful as the new project may sound, you know you are getting overloaded. And that means you must honestly acknowledge the fact that you are reaching your limits. Setting boundaries in this case is really about shifting the schedule or workload.

> *I'm so excited to be given this new assignment. Let's discuss the priorities and schedule so that we can accommodate everything that is currently on my plate. Which of these other projects do you want me to stop working on, so I can join you on the new project?*

> *Who else can we engage in this project or my other projects, in order to accommodate the schedule?*

Can we reshuffle some of our other priorities and deadlines to meet the team's needs without burning everyone out? How can we reach our goals together?

When someone invites you to serve on a committee and you feel pressed for time

Thank you for thinking of me for that committee. I'd love to be involved. I will be finished with this current project in two weeks. May I reconnect with you then to discuss this further?

Exercise

Write your ideas for communicating that you need to offload some of your work. Use the examples above if they help to convey your message. Role play with your accountability partner or a friend.

_____

_____

_____

_____

_____

_____

_____

_____

Think about what you would like to change about your work priorities or schedule. Write down your ideas about how to ask for what you want and need. What words or phrases can you use to make you more comfortable and able to stick to your boundaries? Role play with your accountability partner.

_____

_____

_____

_____

_____

_____

_____

_____

Express Yourself

It is incumbent upon you to express your needs at work and at home. Neither your boss nor your teammates know what you are thinking or feeling if you do not tell them. Similarly, your family members do not know what you are thinking if you say nothing. Sometimes we tend to "act out" with passive-aggressive behavior. That does not count as communicating. No one can read your mind.

Dr. Larry Schooler, conflict resolution consultant and mediator, reminds us that it is important to communicate how you are feeling so that you don't get bottled up with emotions. Simple statements like:

"I feel anger" or *"I feel frustrated"*

clearly articulate that you are bothered by something. Schooler goes on to share that sometimes it is a good idea to wait to respond until you calm down a bit. The more time you give yourself to figure out what you are feeling and why, the more likely your response will yield your desired results, to be listened to, acknowledged, and understood.

This is another situation where ***STOP and AUDIT*** (**Tool #1**) come into play. When you are having an angry reaction to something that has happened, first know that anger is a normal human reaction. However, you may not want to unleash all the vehemence that anger can bring, especially at work. So **STOPPING** helps you acknowledge to yourself what you are feeling, and then the **Stress Audit** helps you connect to exactly what you are feeling.

Once you've figured out what's really bothering you, you often will realize that you can communicate whatever you need to say to the other person. Something like,

I was angry yesterday when you _____ because I _____ .

I would like to _____. Or I would like you to _____ ."

This last part would be about communicating what you validly want or need from the other person.

Here are some "go to" phrases you can use to express your needs in an effective way:

It bothers me when...

It would be helpful if...

Could you please _____ when _____ ?

Examples

It bothers me when *you criticize my work without including any positive reinforcement or any constructive suggestions.* *It would be helpful if* *you include the positives you see in my performance.*

Could you please *offer some positive feedback* *when* *you review my work?*

It bothers me when *you ignore my suggestions without any explanation.*

It would be helpful if *you gave me a little warning or advance notice before dropping a huge task on me with a short deadline.*

When possible, *could you please* *give me more than 24 hours' notice* *when* *you need something done?*

Exercise

Think of times when you felt overwhelmed or like you were beginning to burn out in the past. Pay attention to whether or not you are feeling that way now. Practice writing a few statements to express your needs, using the phrases shown in the examples above or others you can think of. Role play with a buddy or accountability partner.

It bothers me when... _____

_____

_____

Could you please... _____

_____

_____

when... _____

_____

_____

It would be helpful to me if... _____

_____

_____

_____

_____

Ask for Feedback

Sometimes just getting some acknowledgement goes a long way towards reducing your stress and avoiding the feeling of burnout. When your manager writes a personal email to thank you for going the extra mile, it shows the boss cares, appreciates you, and is thinking of you. Your manager may not know what kind of positive reinforcement appeals to you. If you can't communicate this information during the regular course of work, consider bringing it up at review time. Also don't be afraid to let your boss know when he or she tells you about a problem, that you would like some positive feedback to balance the criticism, as discussed in the previous section.

In order for feedback to be effective, it has to be delivered in a form that specifically suits your personality and work style. It won't do much good for your manager to thank you for a job well done by giving you a gift card to a steak house if you're a vegetarian. Also a generic thank you email to 500 people may not feel genuine. As with all of the work you do to set healthy boundaries, it's up to you to identify your needs and then communicate them. Below you'll see some examples of different types of feedback.

Examples

Workplace acknowledgements and positive reinforcement can take many forms. Which do you prefer?

- A figurative pat on the back
- Positive reinforcement or a personally written letter of thanks
- Personal meeting to give feedback
- Acknowledgement in front of other staff members or at an office celebration
- Gift card to your favorite coffee shop, bookstore or other establishment
- Extra mentoring or training to set you up for a desired promotion

Exercise

Think about your desired form of feedback and positive reinforcement. Write your ideas below.

_____

_____

_____

_____

_____

_____

How and when could you communicate the form of feedback you need? You may want to role play with your accountability partner.

_____

_____

_____

_____

_____

Set Limits at Home

Saying *no* to friends and family members is one of the hardest lessons to learn and yet one of the most important parts of self-care and setting healthy boundaries to manage stress. Once I learned how to say *no* I was so much happier. Saying *no* to a friend will not end the friendship. If it does, that person was not a real friend to begin with. Be careful, you may start saying *no* to everyone every day! It's almost too simple.

Friends <u>do</u> take *no* for an answer. Being a good friend means not always having to say *yes*. Just because a friend asks you to do something does not mean there is not someone else who could do it. Of course, there are exceptions. Family members often get a pass, but again, not always. When your partner asks you to do something, when they could just as easily take care of it themselves, do you always say *yes?* Often what they want can wait a few minutes or even a few hours.

At first, setting this type of boundary will be hard for the people in your life to accept, but they will learn to adjust. Sometimes, it's a matter of time, and you can always say this:

"I can help you later, but not now." Or "Let me think about it, and I'll get back to you."

Practice saying *no* without extra explaining, complaining, or self-pity. When you begin to explain why you can't do something, the other person may take that opportunity to try to help you with your obstacles or schedule, so that you can do what they want. In sales, that is called "handling objections." Remember, "No" is a complete sentence.

Example

Your friend texts you on a Friday night asking you to come help them with their garage sale the next morning at 8 am. After a hard week at work, that is the last thing you want to do, wake up early, but this is a good friend. What would you do?

If you need the time to rest, it is perfectly okay to say, "I'd be happy to help with your garage sale, but I will not be available until noon." Or, "I'm so sorry, I wish I could, but I just can't." You need not make any extra explanations.

At first you may feel guilty and buckle under, especially if the friend pushes back. But summon all your strength to politely say *no*.

One additional consideration would be that if this friend is often doing you favors, then you may want to say *yes,* but don't feel guilty about controlling the time.

Exercise

Write out how you would say no to someone in your family or to a friend who wants you to do something that you either do not want to do or feel you should not have to do?

_____

_____

_____

_____

_____

_____

_____

Set Limits with Yourself

Sometimes our pressure emanates from within. You may feel so passionate about your work that you never know when to stop and take a break. Many professionals experience this feeling, including C-suite executives, entrepreneurs, coaches, writers, software developers, graphic artists, advertising executives, lawyers, accountants, and more. It can happen in any profession, especially when you are especially stimulated by your work.

High functioning creatives are often very driven and don't know how to budget their time and more importantly, their energy. They also tend to take on more than they can reasonably handle and will work late into the night to finish everything on their list. It's important to not set unrealistic expectations for yourself.

The purpose of this section is to help you gain the feeling of control over your life, and to help you say *no* to yourself when appropriate.

To begin to access that feeling of control, ask yourself: "What can I reasonably get done today?" Obviously, the word "reasonably" is subjective. So, you may want to work with an accountability partner or your manager on this question. Your manager can help you define a reasonable workload.

A practical tool for seeing if you are trying to accomplish too much in too little time is a planner, be it online, a paper-based notebook or calendar book. Make a daily "power list." Activities can be organized into two main categories. There are **projects,** and within each project there are **tasks**. Make a list of your projects and the most important tasks that have to get done and put the most difficult or time-critical first. Limit your list to no more than three to five major tasks each day. Project Planning pages have been included in the next section, **Manage Your Projects: Plan Your Time**.

Some people find it useful to write a schedule in chunks of 50 or 60 minutes. It is important, as mentioned in the earlier section, *"Combat Stressful "Shoulds"* **(Tool # 2)**, to take a break every hour or between each task. That might mean a five-minute walk around the home-office or workplace. It might mean five minutes of stretching by your desk or taking a walk or jog around the block to the kitchen to get a glass of water. If you are working in an office, try to stop and say a brief *hello* to whomever you run into. Social connectedness is a key to happiness. Even when I work remotely, I periodically visit the other members of my family for a quick hello or a laugh.

But how do you figure out if you really have time to do what you feel you must do? How do you set healthy boundaries for yourself? It depends on your priorities. And those priorities are not just set for one day, but also for the week, month, and year, or for whatever project you've committed to or been assigned. According to Neen James in her book, *Attention Pays*, "you only have time to do what matters."

> # "You only have time to do what matters."
> # — Neen James

Business meetings are another area where you may need to use your power to say *no*. Many executives and employees complain that meetings eat up too much time and are often a waste. Again, Neen James reminds us that you can turn down some meeting invitations. "First, determine if it's necessary for you to attend," she says. Then she goes on to advise that it is wise to ask for the agenda up front. If there isn't one, chances are you shouldn't attend. Also, you may need to attend only the part of the meeting that directly applies to your project. Finally, James advises to "question the purpose of the meeting and how you would add value."

The other huge time waster is emails. James advises reading emails in 15-minute increments, three times per day. Prioritize your emails and give them your full attention but only for 15 minutes. Set a timer and stick to it. This one step will help alleviate some of the stress you feel about managing your time and will boost productivity and focus.

Finally, James suggests putting your phone in *airplane* mode when you have an urgent deadline or just want to minimize distractions.

Example

Do you ever think that you can catch up with your work on the weekend? Does that project or assignment really have to be finished by Monday? If not, consider taking the weekend off. Taking a break is an important part of self-care. It helps you decompress from the prior week and get rejuvenated for the week to come, so you can be your most productive self during the week.

Do you ever put pressure on yourself to take on one more volunteer activity just because someone asked you to, and you feel it's a really good cause? We often get caught up in the moment without maintaining perspective on all our other responsibilities.

Exercise

When you are tempted to work on the weekend, due to pressure from yourself, try answering the following question: *What will happen if I let go of my work this weekend? How will I feel after having a weekend of needed rest, relaxation, and fun?*

_____

_____

_____

_____

_____

_____

_____

_____

_____

Manage Your Projects: Plan Your Time

As described in the preceding sections there can be many demands on your time at work or at home.

Time management can be a huge source of stress, usually because you are overloaded, or you place too many demands on yourself. You may simply need help managing your time. Time management skills can help you reduce the emotional burden of being disorganized with your time.

Can you remember the last time you felt overwhelmed because you had a huge project that made you feel nervous or stressed? Or maybe you felt overwhelmed because you simply had too many items on your "to do" list, or because everything on your list seemed equally important.

Suddenly you procrastinated because the very idea of the project overwhelmed you, and you didn't know where to start.

Whatever major project you have to do, the best way to take control over it and your nerves is to break it into smaller chunks and prioritize them. Every major *project* has parts or *tasks*, that often have to be done in a certain order. One of the keys is knowing where to start and how you will proceed.

Planning your time is a form of self-care that must be designed to suit your individual needs and personality. Have you ever noticed how you feel after completing a huge task, like cleaning out your closet? Every time you complete a difficult or large project or task, your brain gets flooded with a happiness chemical, dopamine.

In terms of time management systems, you might have more success with one type over another. You may like to keep a list of major projects or tasks on paper on your desk. Some people like a wall calendar for planning, while others keep everything on their phone or computer. And others keep a whiteboard on their wall with projects across the top and the list of tasks underneath each. The main objective in planning your projects and your time is to find a system that works well for you that will best help you get and stay organized.

In the first section below, you'll find a simple strategy for planning your time for a day. Then in the **Project Management** section we will move on to a more detailed discussion about how to manage two different types of projects: **one-person** and **multi-person**.

To begin, you'll see two examples and exercises that will help you focus on setting daily priorities and accomplishing them. Even though your "to do" list may run for several pages, there is only so much you can actually accomplish in any one workday. In this exercise, you choose the top three to five items that are actually achievable and that will produce the most results and satisfaction when completed. Then you will have another option for plotting out each hour of the day. You will need to decide which plan works best for you.

Example

By the end of the day, I will feel satisfied and less stressed if I accomplish these tasks:

1. *Finish first draft of the report due next week.*
2. *Schedule user interviews for my software development project.*
3. *Plan and organize presentation to management due in two weeks*
4. *Time permitting, start to write out the presentation*
5. *Time permitting, practice the presentation.*

> **"Always think, 'What most needs my attention at this moment?' when asking to shift priorities."**
> **— Neen James**

Exercise

Think about the three to five tasks you would like to complete in one day and write them below.

Say to yourself, "By the end of the day, I will feel satisfied if I accomplish these tasks." Consider putting your least favorite or most challenging item first, so that you can get it out of the way and feel really satisfied after completion.

Task List

1. _____

2. _____

3. _____

4. _____

5. _____

Planning a Day with a Schedule for Structure

Some people find it helpful to put a structure around their day. The table below shows an example of a typical day for me. It doesn't always flow as perfectly as I've outlined it here, however it gives me an overall structure for the day and keeps me on track.

Time	Activity
9:00 – 9:15	EMAIL
9:15 – 10:15	Write Introduction for ***Banish Burnout Toolkit***
10:20 – 11:20	Respond to Jenny W. (client), who requested information about customizing my ***Banish Burnout: Move from Stress to Success*** workshop
11:30 – 12:30	Collaborate with speaker, Joe S. on *Self-Care Virtual Presentation*
12:30 – 1:30	Lunch & walk (if possible, invite a friend)
1:30 – 2:30	Zoom Meeting with wellness mentee
2:35 – 3:35	LinkedIn Communication including responding to messages and connection requests, considering an article to share or thinking about a new blog post.
3:40 – 4:00	EMAIL
4:00 – 5:00	Time permitting: Catch-up or other Zoom calls

Notice how I build in a 5-minute break roughly after each hour and a walk after lunch.

If I have extra time, I may make more marketing phone calls or emails, plan a blog post or newsletter, plan a book launch event, network with other wellness professionals, coaches, or speakers, or study the latest workplace wellness research.

Sometimes all I really need is a block of two to four hours to complete some tasks, and then I open up the rest of the day to Zoom meetings.

Exercise

If you like the idea of plotting out your day with specific hours, try writing a schedule. Remember to allow time for breaks and some physical activity either during the day or after work.

9:00	
10:00	
11:00	
12:00	
1:00	
2:00	
3:00	
4:00	
5:00	

Project Management

A project differs from an operational task, such as running the payroll, which is done every week, because a project has a beginning, middle, and end. One of the keys to planning your time is knowing where to start and how you will proceed throughout the timeframe of the project.

There are two types of projects described in this section. The first is a **one-person project** or your own piece of a bigger project, and it primarily involves only your time, and perhaps that of an assistant. The second is a **multi-person project**, a major effort with many steps involving various people, resources, and a larger budget.

Examples of the **one-person project** include interviewing users for a software development project, writing a book, completing a report, doing the taxes, developing a plan for a website, writing a speech, organizing sales leads, or marketing using social media.

Examples of the **multi-person project** include planning a major event, developing a major piece of software or hardware, auditing a corporate department, developing a sales plan, or designing and implementing a wellness program.

As an individual employee, using the tools in the one-person project section will probably be most helpful, while the multi-person project section will be of interest to managers and team leaders.

One-Person Project

This section will help you learn how to plan and manage your work, control your time, and begin to recognize how much you can really accomplish in one day. Eventually your estimation of time will be more and more accurate.

Whether you are self-employed or working as part of a team effort, some experts recommend

making a "power list" of up to five tasks or pieces of a bigger project. Try to make sure you are not biting off more than you can chew. For example, while I was working on this book, it was hard to get other items done during the day. So, I had to break this book project into smaller chunks in order to accomplish other important tasks. You can see how I might organize a typical day in the previous section.

Example

In my experience I have found the following steps to be most useful when setting up a vibrant, all-inclusive wellness program:

1. Develop a first draft budget based on researching other organizations of a similar size.[1]
2. Meet with leaders to get commitment and agree on a budget. If you sense that there will be resistance, I recommend bringing a committed leader and arming yourself with wellness success stories.[2]
3. Recruit wellness champions from around the company.
4. Survey employees to determine wellness goals. Short surveys work well.
5. Meet with wellness champions to brainstorm ideas and begin to create a calendar. Remember to incorporate ideas from all five tenets of wellness: physical heath, mental health, financial, social, and communication.[3]
6. Track results to measure effectiveness. Areas of measurement would include participation, absentee rates, improvements in health care costs, as well as individual employees' sense of improved wellness.[4]

Exercise

Make a list of major projects you are working on right now. Underneath each project list all the major tasks that apply, in order of importance, and note their deadlines, and any project dependencies. If the project is for yourself, or you are self-employed and don't have an official deadline, you might want to set artificial deadlines for each part of the project to give yourself some structure. Remember the best way to attack a large project is to break it into smaller, doable chunks.

Each day create a to-do list for the day, keeping in mind your project priorities, and what you can truly accomplish in one day. Remember to put the least pleasant or most difficult task first. At the end of each day, go back and think about how accurate or inaccurate your estimates were so you can plan better in the future. Also relish in the good feelings of accomplishment each day.

In combination with the **Project-Task Planner** below, you might want to incorporate either the

Task List and/or the **Hourly Task Planner** (each illustrated earlier in this Tool).

Project-Task List Planner

Project #1:   Due Date:

Task 1:	Due:
Task 2:	Due:
Task 3:	Due:
Task 4:	Due:
Task 5:	Due:

Project #2:   Due Date:

Task 1:	Due:
Task 2:	Due:
Task 3:	Due:
Task 4:	Due:
Task 5:	Due:

Project #3:   **Due Date:**

Task 1:   Due:

Task 2:   Due:

Task 3:   Due:

Task 4:   Due:

Task 5:   Due:

Project #4:   **Due Date:**

Task 1:   Due:

Task 2:   Due:

Task 3:   Due:

Task 4:   Due:

Task 5:   Due:

Project #5:   **Due Date:**

Task 1:   Due:

Task 2:   Due:

Task 3:   Due:

Task 4:   Due:

Task 5:   Due:

Some people find it useful to plot out an hour-by-hour schedule, as I did in my *typical day* example previously, building in breaks, big tasks, and yes, even exercise. Planners and calendars for that kind of schedule are available almost anywhere you like to buy your office supplies, or as stated previously, you can make your own.

Multi-Person Project

What if you are a team lead or project manager for a major project at work?

When you are first starting out as a project manager, estimating time for projects can seem daunting. Project time estimation gets easier with experience. Use your best judgment to make an educated guess, and then ask all key stakeholders including the project team to review and comment. According to Susan Schwartz, executive and organizational coach, trainer, and author of *Creating a Greater Whole: A Project Manager's Guide to Becoming a Leader*, the key to being a good manager is to set expectations, prioritize, and communicate these expectations to your team. In the References section you will find project estimation templates.[5]

In general, the multi-person project would include a number of resources, people, and budgets. It might involve a project like planning an event, building a house, designing and developing a piece of software or app, or developing a piece of hardware or gadget, such as a new iPhone, preparing for a legal trial, or any other major undertaking.

Here are the steps for project planning and execution.

Step 1: Purpose

What is the **purpose** of the project and who are all the key **stakeholders** or **clients**? Describe the purpose in one or two sentences. This is also known as a **Statement of Work**.

Think about all of the possible players that would benefit from the project.

Step 2: Deliverables

What is / are the **deliverable**(s)?

Examples: a piece of software, a new company website, or a financial plan for a client.

Step 3: Deadline

What is the overall project deadline?

If you don't have a hard and fast deadline, when would you like it to be done?

Note: Often clients push for a deadline that you think may be unreasonable. Follow your gut. Do not commit to a deadline that you are not 100% comfortable with. If they push hard then negotiate the removal of any piece that would help you meet their deadline. Alternatively, you can agree to the deadline in exchange for a bigger budget due to the need for increased personnel. If necessary, include an advocate or manager in the negotiation.

Step 4: Phases

Write the overall **project plan**, listing out every **major section** and all the **interdependencies,** which dictate the order. For example, a software, hardware, or construction project cannot move from one step to the next until the prior step is completed. You cannot begin to build the walls of a house or building until the foundation is laid.

Step 5: Tasks

List all the tasks or steps, in order, for each major section.

Step 6: Resources

Designate, gather, and allocate required resources, tools, **or information,** such as project team members and raw materials, supplies, or equipment. Obviously if you are building a house, you need cement, bricks, nails, etc. If you are developing software, you need staff, hardware time, or maybe new equipment.

Step 7: Estimates

Estimate how long each section or task will take.

Remember, always allow extra time for unexpected developments.

A personal note: I once worked as a software support consultant and had to estimate many development projects. My boss taught me that you can never plan for every eventuality, so add 50% for "good measure." You never know when one of the key team members may get sick.

So, allowing for the unexpected helps you and your project stay on track. When in doubt, ask a mentor or your manager for advice. Over time you will get better at estimating time.

Step 8: Start Date

Determine start date. When does the project have to start in order to meet your deadline? This date is figured by starting with the deadline and working backwards in time, taking each task's time allotment into account.

Step 9: Budget

Estimate costs and write a budget. Of course, this depends on whether you are writing a time and materials or flat fee budget. It would depend on the practices of your organization and the vendors you rely upon.

Ask yourself, if the allocated funds are enough to complete the project within the deadline and level of quality required. Do not guess. Get help from a manager or the PMI website[5]. The cost estimate is often placed in a Proposal Addendum.

Step 10: Execution

Execute the plan and document how much actual time each task took and how much of the funds were used, and report to accounting, as required by your organization.

This review will help you recognize realistic time schedules and monies needed for the future.

A personal note: Years ago, my mother taught me to always sleep on a project, be it a proposal, a paper, a speech or even your taxes. The reason for this is that after you are finished, your brain begins to relax and ideas you omitted pop into your head the day after. So, allowing an extra day gives new or forgotten ideas a chance to flow. Even though these steps may seem obvious, writing them down helps you plan your time.

For further support, use the resources of the Project Management Institute (PMI).

To help you plan, the Project Management Institute website offers project planning templates and other resources. These templates will help you estimate costs and statistically estimate project uncertainties.[5]

Set Healthy Boundaries

Tool #6:
Enlist an Accountability Partner

Several times in the previous pages I have referenced the idea of engaging an accountability partner or buddy for guidance. This is the sixth and final piece of the **Banish Burnout Toolkit.** This person should be someone you trust deeply and with whom you can share your frustrations as well as celebrations.

I cannot stress enough the importance of an accountability buddy, mentor, or best friend at work. In *Permission to Feel*, Marc Brackett stresses that "social support has been demonstrated to be a highly effective buffer against the adverse effects of stress, due to its influence on promoting healthy behaviors." Brackett goes on to point out that social support can affect your health.

The work you do with the tools in this workbook will be more effective when you engage with a partner who will hold you accountable and guide you. Sometimes when we get stuck in our own head, it's hard to see clearly. I am reminded of the metaphor of not being able to see the forest for the trees.

Your accountability partner is there to challenge you and help you become aware of your responses to stress and the ways you manage or fail to manage it. Having built-in support can help keep you on track with setting your boundaries and your limits. A partner can also help you determine what steps to take when you're beginning to feel burned out, whom to approach and how to approach them.

That is why it is ideal to choose someone from within your organization. They can be a "best friend at work." If you are unable to engage a dependable buddy in your workplace, you can find or choose someone from outside your company, a trusted friend or mentor.

Humans are wired for social connection. The happiness chemical, oxytocin is released when we connect with a close friend or trusted confidante. We just feel better. Not only that, being close to others pays off in other ways as well. Bill Gates, in fact, has stated that the feeling of connection and belonging is critical to his success.[1]

In a report entitled "Why We need Best Friends at Work,"[2] Gallup found that 63 percent of people who have a best friend in their workplace are twice as engaged in their work. Otherwise, without a colleague in the company to commiserate with, work can seem lonely and isolating.

Having a best friend at work is particularly important if you work in a high-stress environment. For example, let's say you really want to go to the fitness center, but you feel overwhelmed with your workload. Armed with a well-thought-out daily plan (as described in **Tool #5**) and a best friend to exercise with, you would be more likely to take the time to go to that fun Zumba class or relaxing Yoga class you really enjoy if you knew your friend planned to meet you there. As a result, you experience not only the oxytocin release described above, but also the endorphins from the exercise, a double whammy of happiness chemicals. Furthermore, you'll feel refreshed from having taken a break from your work.

Photo by Y-Boychenko on DepositPhotos.com. Used under Standard License.

You might also consider doing role play exercises with your partner, as referenced in earlier sections. For instance, if you need practice talking to your manager about re-assigning excess projects or asking for something else you need or want, you could play out the scenario with your accountability buddy so you will be better prepared for the actual conversation with your manager.

One way to work with your accountability partner is to set a regular meeting day with the added commitment that you'll be available for each other on an as-needed basis. Whomever you choose, make sure that person has the time and the capability to work with you. By that I mean, it might make sense to encourage them to work through the ***Banish Burnout Toolkit*** with you.

Example

Kamal wanted help setting boundaries at work and getting more exercise. He enlisted Thomas, a friend who worked in another department, to meet with him once a week. The two buddies used their lunch break to walk to a nearby park and discuss Kamal's goals and challenges, while eating their lunch. Thomas also agreed to check Kamal's "to do" list via email every few days to help keep him on track with his many projects and tasks.

Exercise

Use the space below to answer the following questions about working with an accountability buddy.

Think about your ideal accountability buddy. Ask yourself: "Do I need someone just to listen and offer gentle suggestions, or someone who will challenge me to stretch?" Think about what type of schedule will work for you, keeping in mind that your potential partners may have limited availability and you may have to bend to their schedule.

Now make a list of people who might make an appropriate accountability buddy for you. Set a date to begin contacting potential partners.

_____

_____

_____

_____

_____

If you have identified someone you know fairly well, then you probably don't need help asking them. However, if you do not know them well and need help crafting a request, here is a sample email.

> Dear Joe:
>
> *I am working on the goal of managing my stress better and controlling my workflow and schedule. I was wondering if you might be interested and available to work with me on these goals. We could meet weekly if that works for your schedule. Please let me know if you would be interested and have the time.*

It is critical to be respectful of other people's time. If you think this person is very busy, I recommend putting a limit on the number of meetings and the amount of time for each in the request. For example, you could ask for four meetings of 30 – 60 minutes each.

Don't be afraid to ask for help. People like helping other people and have gotten help themselves along the way. If they are not available, they will let you know. Enlisting help from a coach or accountability partner is one of the best ways you can grow your career and understand what steps you need to get there. Go for it. You'll be glad you did.

Access an Accountability Partner

Additional Notes

Additional Notes

Conclusion

Your boss and your company do not want you to burn out!

All the parts of the ***Banish Burnout Toolkit*** add up to an important set of tools to combat stress and prevent burnout. The **Stress Audit** combined with all of the other tools and reality checks help you to identify your own patterns of behavior, including the genesis of those behavior patterns, so that you can effect real behavior change. Then the self-care, healthy boundary and accountability partner tools help you think about your future.

> # You cannot take care of your work, your team, or your family, if you do not take care of yourself!

Keep your *Banish Burnout Toolkit* close at hand at all times as a cue, to pick it up whenever you have a stressful event. My wish for you is that you find deep knowledge and value from working the toolkit.

Please let me know how you are doing with it from time to time. I always welcome success stories and questions. Connect with me any time on your favorite social media channel or via email.

Ways to Keep in Touch:

Linkedin: Open your camera to scan my **Linkedin QR Code**, and you will instantly find my profile.

Instagram: @JaniceLitvin

Facebook: Janice Litvin Speaks

Twitter: @JLitvin

YouTube: Janice Litvin

References

Tool #4: Practice Self-Care

Get Adequate Sleep

1. Wellness Council of America. (2008). A good night's sleep: Stress, insomnia and productivity.
2. Press and Resources - The Sleep Ambassador®. (2020, July 31). Retrieved September 02, 2020, from http://thesleepambassador.com/resources/

Go Outside

1. Christensen, B. (2014, February 21). Morning light relieves anxiety. Retrieved September 02, 2020, from https://sciencenordic.com/a/1397274
2. Sprouse, S. (2018, February 26). 10 Reasons Why Being Outside is Important. Retrieved September 02, 2020, from https://askthescientists.com/outdoors/
3. Boosting Your Serotonin Activity. (2011, November 17). Retrieved September 02, 2020, from https://www.psychologytoday.com/us/blog/prefrontal-nudity/201111/boosting-your-serotonin-activity
4. Ornes, S. (2019, December 03). Sunlight makes pleasure chemical in the body. Retrieved September 02, 2020, from https://www.sciencenewsforstudents.org/article/sunlight-makes-pleasure-chemical-body
5. Sprouse, S. (2018, February 26). 10 Reasons Why Being Outside is Important. Retrieved September 02, 2020, from https://askthescientists.com/outdoors/

Tool #5: Set Healthy Boundaries

Manage Your Projects: Plan Your Time

1. There is a wealth of information at any of the wellness associations, including WELCOA (Wellness Council of America), Art and Science of Health Promotion Institute, HERO (The Health Enhancement Research Organization) National Wellness Institute, NBGH (National Business Group on Health), Medical Wellness Association, Centers for Disease Control – Workplace Health Promotion, Corporate Health & Wellness Association, etc.
2. Purcell, J. (2019, July 09). How To Engage CEOs In Employee Well-Being. Retrieved September 02, 2020, from https://www.forbes.com/sites/jimpurcell/2019/06/24/how-to-engage-ceos-in-employee-wellbeing/

3. Mitchell, T., Straub, P. Allen, R., & Roberts, T. (2020). *104 challenges: Become the best you.* Chicago, IL:WellRight. Free download can be found at: https://www.wellright.com/wellness-resources/books

4. According to one wellness expert, Dee Eddington, PhD, it takes two or more years to see results in health care spending from a wellness program. Eddington, D. (n.d.). Retrieved September 02, 2020, from http://edingtonassociates.com/

5. *See also* Project Management Institute, www.pmi.org or https://www.projectmanagement.com/Templates

Tool #6: Enlist an Accountability Partner

1. Schwantes, M. (2020, April 06). Bill Gates Says He Now Asks Himself 1 Crucial Question He Would Not Have Asked in His Microsoft Days. Retrieved September 02, 2020, from https://www.inc.com/marcel-schwantes/bill-gates-says-he-now-asks-himself-1-crucial-question-he-would-not-have-asked-in-his-microsoft-days.html

2. Mann, A. (2020, May 05). Why We Need Best Friends at Work. Retrieved September 02, 2020, from https://www.gallup.com/workplace/236213/why-need-best-friends-work.aspx

Acknowledgements

There are several people without whom I would not have been able to write this book.

Mary Claire Blakeman, my unending supporter beyond editing. She might be advising about office organization or anything else that would help me finish my writing projects. More important, she is insightful and intuitive and just plain smart, an all-around excellent developmental editor.

Amy Waninger, for her calm and supportive demeanor and excellent skills, as I tried to navigate the waters of book design and publishing.

Dr. Elayne Savage, practicing psychotherapist, workplace coach and trainer, and author of *Don't Take It Personally! The Art of Dealing with Rejection*, for her support on **Tool #3: Unpack Your Emotional Baggage.**

Nancy Rothstein, MBA, The Sleep Ambassador®, for her input on the *Get Adequate Sleep* section.

Dr. Larry Schooler, conflict resolution consultant, mediator, and facilitator, for his support on the *Express Yourself* section.

Neen James, professional speaker and author of *Attention Pays,* for her input in the **Manage Your Projects: Plan Your Time** section.

Susan Schwartz, executive and organizational coach, trainer, and author of *Creating a Greater Whole: A Project Manager's Guide to Becoming a Leader,* for her expert advice about project management in the **Manage Your Projects: Plan Your Time** section.

To the many supporters and advisors who have offered advice, feedback, and reinforcement for my **Banish Burnout: Move from Stress to Success** program, which was the genesis of this workbook. You are too numerous to mention here, but I appreciate each and every one of you.

To my family, including my loving and supportive husband, **Joseph Litvin**, and my son, **Lee Litvin**, the entrepreneur, rapper (aka *Leezythegifted*), music producer, and basketball coach. Thank you both for your undying support, advice and your deep insights.

Posthumously to **Dr. Albert Ellis** (1913 – 2007), American psychologist, author of *The Practice of Rational Emotive Behavior Therapy* and many other books, without whose pioneering work in Cognitive Behavior Therapy, this workbook and program would not be possible.

About the Author

Janice Litvin is on a mission to help leaders and teams banish burnout in their organizations. She does this through keynotes, workshops, and accountability groups.

As an award-winning speaker, certified virtual speaker, and official SHRM Recertification Provider, she wants to help as many people as possible take care of their physical and mental health, including teaching them to manage stress to prevent burnout, to eat healthfully, and to fall in love with fitness. In these ways, she is

helping people change their lives. She has developed unique strategies to maximize engagement in workplace wellness and has also developed a stress management methodology available through her workbook, *Banish Burnout Toolkit*.

What makes Janice unique is that in addition to 20 years as a technology recruiter, ten years of IT experience, and her studies of psychology, she has overcome all the challenges she teaches about in her presentations. She went from being overweight and sedentary with a critical, negative attitude to a lighter, fitter, happier person who now teaches Zumba Fitness and leads stress management and healthy eating workshops and accountability groups. She is certified by the Aerobics and Fitness Association of America.

After forming Micro Search in 1983 to help clients learn how to manage their business using a desktop computer, she became a human resource executive technology recruiter in response to her Fortune 500 clients' needs for technology talent. Over the next twenty years, clients included Charles Schwab, Oracle, The Gap, Computer Partners, Network Appliance, QuinStreet, Symantec, Vodafone, Chiron, TheraSense, Nokia, Borland, United States Army, Pacific Gas & Electric and Pacific Bell.

Janice has served on the Workplace Wellness Committee of the American Heart Association and spoken on their behalf to San Francisco Bay Area organizations. She is a member of the National Speakers Association, WELCOA (Wellness Council of America), and SHRM Northern California (Society for Human Resource Management). In 2017 she formed the Bay Area Wellness Association.

In addition to SHRM Nor Cal, Janice has worked with a range of other clients to present wellness workshops and programs, including PIHRA (Professionals in Human Resources Association), CAL SAE (California Society of Association Executives), Meetings Today, Coral Reef Alliance, San Mateo Unified High School District, WellRight, HR Southwest, Minnesota State SHRM Council, NCHRA (Next Concept Human Resources Association), First Republic Bank, Robert Half, Cities of Walnut Creek and Sunnyvale, and US HHS.

Book Janice to Speak

Training Topics

- Banish Burnout: Move from Stress to Success
- Innovations in Workplace Wellness
- Fall in Love with Fitness
- Lose for Life: How to Keep the Weight Off for Life

Ask me about my accountability programs!

If you are aware of any organizations that would benefit from a workshop based on the **Banish Burnout Toolkit**, or any of my other topics, please get in touch at Janice@JaniceLitvin.com or (415) 518-2202. More information and videos are available at: www.JaniceLitvin.com.

Janice Litvin
Wellness Speaker

www.JaniceLitvin.com
Janice@JaniceLitvin.com
415.518.2202

Made in the USA
Middletown, DE
18 May 2023

30845622R00058